THE MOTHER GOOSE MYSTERIES

HIDDEN HISTORY

"Whereas the truth is that when we read *Mother Goose* aloud to the family, we are commenting on whole pages of English history. No one seems to have attempted to assemble and set down the origin of popular traditional verse; such knowledge has to be slowly accumulated by hearsay or accidental discovery. What does "Hey diddle, diddle, the cat and the fiddle" mean? Where was the "House that Jack built?" And so on for scores of others. It is high time that those who search back into the social side of English history should pool their information.

Lady Maxse, Editor of the *National Review*, September 1941

This book is dedicated to all those who came to my 80th birthday party on 28th July 2024.

First published 2024 by Susak Press
daniel@susakpress.com

10 9 8 7 6 5 4 3 2 1

Text © 2024 Tim Devlin
Illustrations © 2024 Katarina Dragoslavić

The right of Tim Devlin and Katarina Dragoslavić to be identified as the author and illustrator respectively of this work has been asserted by them in accordance with the Copyright, Designs and Patents Act 1988

This book has been typeset in Abadi MT Pro

Printed in UK by CLOC

All rights reserved. No part of this book may be reproduced, transmitted or stored in an information retrieval system in any form or by any means, graphic, electronic or mechanical, including photocopying, taping and recording, without prior written permission from the publisher.

ISBN 978-1-3999-8573-4

THE MOTHER GOOSE MYSTERIES

AN INVESTIGATIVE TRAIL OF FAVOURITE NURSERY RHYMES

by Tim Devlin

illustrations by
Katarina Dragoslavić

TIM DEVLIN – former journalist and education correspondent of *The Times*, is co-author of books on what we should teach in schools, famous people and where they went to school, and a real murder mystery in his home county of Sussex where he now lives. He was educated at Winchester College and Oxford University where he studied history. He is married with four grown-up children and six grand-children and spends some of his time crocheting presents for friends and family and hat bases for the long-running musical *The Lion King*.

www.humptycracked.com
@humptycracked @men_should_crochet

KATARINA DRAGOSLAVIĆ is an illustrator and designer of children's books and has worked for leading publishers. She grew up in Croatia where she studied graphic design in Pula and then studied Fine Art at the academies of Bologna and Macerata in Italy. She came to England in 1998 and worked as a graphic designer for various Children's Books publishers. She has an MA in Children's Book Illustration at ARU in Cambridge and won the **2022 Stratford Salariya Children's Picture Book Prize** for her book *The Little Hungry Dinosaur*.

www.katarinadragoslavic.myportfolio.com
@katarina_illustration

design by Susak Press
www.susakpress.com
@susakpress

TABLE OF CONTENTS

Foreword: *Who was Mother Goose?* 7
Notes for readers 12
Main works consulted 14
Chapter 1:
When the inspector didn't call | **Doctor Foster** 17
Chapter 2:
The turbulent priest | **Goosey, Goosey, Gander** 29
Chapter 3:
Found in translation | **Hickory Dickory Dock** 37
Chapter 4:
The proof of the pudding | **Lion And The Unicorn** 43
Chapter 5:
Merry Prankster, prig or thief? | **Little Jack Horner** 51
Chapter 6:
Thomas the Spiderman | **Little Miss Muffet** 63
Chapter 7:
Who was My Fair Lady? | **London Bridge** 71
Chapter 8:
Fundraiser and fake | **Mary Had A Little Lamb** 83
Chapter 9:
Old Mother Wolsey? | **Old Mother Hubbard** 93
Chapter 10:
The dance that went crazy | **Pop Goes The Weasel** 101
Chapter 11:
The Princess and the Statue | **Ride A Cock Horse** 109
Chapter 12:
A dainty royal happy birthday dish | **Sing A Song Of Sixpence** 123
Chapter 13:
Silly fools or brave martyrs? | **Three Blind Mice** 131
Chapter 14:
Nursery Rhyme's Who Dunnit | **Who Killed Cock Robin?** . . . 139
Epilogue: *Old Soldiers Never Die* 151
Appendix: *Clues to the illustrations* 162
Index of names and places 176

FOREWORD

WHO WAS MOTHER GOOSE?

Old Mother Goose
When she wanted to wander
Would ride through the air
On a very fine gander.

Who was Mother Goose? Did she ever exist? This is perhaps the greatest unexplained nursery rhyme mystery. For centuries in America nursery rhymes have been known as Mother Goose rhymes. Also in Britain Lady Maxse, the influential magazine editor writing in 1941, did not refer to 'nursery rhymes' but to 'Mother Goose' as you can see from the 'Hidden History' quote on the very first page of this book.

Why was this story-telling old lady, later the pantomime friend of a fowl that lays golden eggs, ever used as the inventor of jingles which first emerged in printed collections in mid-18th century London? Welcome to *The Mother Goose Mysteries*!

They (the mysteries) begin with a suspect grave in an American cemetery. Here the story-telling dame is still venerated in Boston, Massachusetts. Boston's Freedom Trail follows the steps of the patriot silversmith and watchman Paul Revere whose midnight ride on horseback in April 1775 alerted America to the advance of British troops. It attracts some three million visitors a year.

Often the trail starts at the end of his life with a trek through the old Granary Burying Ground in Tremont Street where the famous revolutionary is buried.

Here also among approximately 2345 graves and tombs is a 26-inch-tall slate slab, topped by a 'death's head' carving in the form of a skull with wings. Below it is a pair of stone-carved crossed bones and four diamond-shaped and circular symbols. And beneath them the inscription reads: "Here lyes y body of Mary Goose, wife to Isaac Goose, aged 42, dec(eased) 1690."

Inspired by travel brochures, nursery rhyme pilgrims travel from far and wide to throw coins onto her grave.

In the year 2000 Kelly Thomas started and still runs the Historic Burying Grounds Initiative that looks after 16 historic graveyards in the city. She guesses that there could be as many as a million visitors every year to the Granary Burying Ground. She told me: "We do not ask people why they visit it. I have noticed that in my conversations with people, many of them express interest in the 'Mother Goose' stone, so I think it is popular."

But the object of their interest is literally a wild goose chase! Mary Goose was the first wife of a well-to-do Bostonian Isaac Goose (or possibly Vergoose), and her resting-place is one of the greatest examples of posthumous mistaken tomb identity in history. It was the wrong wife. Mary never had anything to do with the publication of nursery rhymes. Elsewhere in a Boston cemetery among the masses of unmarked graves probably lie the remains of one Elizabeth Foster Goose who died in 1757. But not even Kelly Thomas, who knows the location of each headstone and for the past 24 years has been responsible for maintaining and preserving every grave in all 16 burying grounds, knows where to find her.

Elizabeth Foster was born in Charlestown, Massachusetts in 1665. She was 27 when she became widower Isaac Goose's second wife. He was 57 and plainly very fertile. He already had 10 children via Mary and with Elizabeth he had a further six. One of them was also called Elizabeth and she married a Bristol-born publisher Thomas Fleet who had emigrated to America and set up shop in Pudding Lane, Boston.

Elizabeth (the second) and Thomas Fleet also had six children. When Isaac died aged 73 in 1710 Elizabeth (the first) joined the family and came to live in Pudding Lane in rooms over the shop. And it is here that the grandmother, who lived well into her 90s, is supposed to have chanted rhymes to her grandchildren – some from memory and some made up.

The Boyd Smith Mother Goose (1919), one of about two dozen books on the origin of nursery rhymes which I consulted, described how Thomas Fleet, "a man fond of quiet" was at first irritated by the chattering, but then he saw a gap in the market, copied down the verses as his mother-in-law recited them and published them in 1719 as *Songs for the Nursery or Mother Goose*. They sold at his shop for two coppers a piece.

No one heard about this book for another 140 years. Then on 14th January 1860 an article appeared in *The Boston Transcript* under the pen name *Requiescat*. Its author John Fleet Eliot, the great-grandson of Thomas Fleet, claimed that his great-great-grandmother Elizabeth was the real Mother Goose, the 'Mother Goose of Pudding Lane'.

Was he serious or was it all a fake? He could have been making the most of the coincidence that Mother Goose was also the name of a legendary story-telling dame with medieval roots. Gloria Delamar, author of *Mother Goose from Nursery to Literature*, said the dame was a mixture of two Berthas. One was the eighth century mother of the great Frankish Emperor Charlemagne. She was called *La Reine Pédauque* (Queen Goose-foot or 'Bertha Broadfoot) because of the size of her feet which were said to be both large and webbed. The other, more than two centuries later, was another Frankish queen called Bertha wife of Robert II of France (c970-1031). This princess from Burgundy fell foul of two popes (Gregory V and his successor Sylvester II) when in around 996 AD she married her second cousin. Both popes denounced the marriage as being 'incestuous' and the couple were forced to separate but not before they had produced a child. It was rumoured that it came out of the womb with the head of a goose!

Katherine Elwes Thomas, the American nursery rhyme detective, wrote in *The Real Personages of Mother Goose* (1930): "Queen Bertha is represented in French legends as spinning with children clustered about her listening to tales. From this arose the French custom of referring any incredible stories to the 'time when good Queen Bertha spun'."

Tales of the original spin doctor's prowess in telling tall stories and legends survived through the Middle Ages. Andrew Lang, born 1844, a hero of my youth (I loved his different coloured fairy books), discovered the earliest surviving reference to Mother Goose. He spotted a poem printed in a letter in June 1650 by Jean Loret, the journalist, writer and poet, in his weekly Paris newsletter *La Muse Historique*. It contained the following couplet:

> *Comme un conte de la mère oye* [like a story of Mother Goose]
> *Se trouvent fabuleux et faux* [they find fables and fakes].

The second person who propelled Mother Goose into stardom was Charles Perrault, the distinguished French poet, storyteller and member of the Académie Française. He laid the foundations for a new literary genre – the fairy tale. In 1697 he published a collection of tales in Paris under the title *Histoires ou contes du temps passé, avec des moralités*. The stories included *Little Red Riding Hood, Cinderella* and others which are still among the best known today. The title page of the book showed an old woman spinning and telling stories with a notice on the door above her proclaiming: *'Contes De la Mere Oye'*.

Gloria Delamar maintained that this volume of fairy stories "set the stage for the [Mother Goose] name to become a household word". She also did her bit because she had the brilliant idea of an annual Mother Goose Day in the USA every May 1st. It started with the publication of her book (cited above) in 1987.

Perrault's volume of fairy tales was for the first time translated into English by the writer Robert Samber in 1729. The tales were sold in several editions to the British public. One of the publishers who sold them was the printer John Newbery. He was a farmer's son who started his business in Reading, Berkshire, as a provincial bookseller, newspaper proprietor and seller of medicines. He then expanded into children's books as one of many business opportunities and moved to London in 1744.

He soon turned to publishing rhymes and jingles convinced that he was entering a lucrative market. He edited *Mother Goose's Melody or Sonnets for the Cradle* around 1765 – two years before his death. It was registered by his stepson Thomas Carnan at Stationers' Hall, London, in December 1780. It was good value for money costing just threepence. Part 1 contained 52 "celebrated songs and lullabies of the old British nurses". These included many of the oldest nursery rhymes and the first known prints of *Jack and Jill* and *Little Jack Horner*. Part 2 contained 16 songs and lullabies from Shakespeare such as *Where the Bee sucks, there suck I* (from *The Tempest*).

Two giant poets – Mother Goose and William Shakespeare - in one small book! According to the website *rhymes.org.uk* one of the versions of *Mother Goose's Melody* pirated across the Atlantic had a front cover picture of the old crone addressing her children as follows: "We two great poets were born together, and we shall go out of the world together. No, No, my Melodies will never die, while nurses sing, or babies cry." It was a landmark publication. Gloria Delamar wrote: "With his adoption of her name [Mother Goose] for a collection of mostly traditional rhymes, he [John Newbery] usurped her former alliance with the fairy tales."

Until the end of the 18th century Mother Goose was the leading brand for children's nursery rhymes. But then in 1806 Mother Goose embarked on her third career. *Harlequin and Mother Goose or The Golden Egg* opened on Boxing Day at the Theatre

Royal in Covent Garden. It was a 92-night hit grossing £20,000 (nearly £2m in today's money) and starred the great pantomime clown Joseph Grimaldi. Around 1815 a chapbook (a small paper-covered booklet often with crude woodcuts) was published about the goose who laid the golden eggs. The first verse quoted at the head of this chapter begins: *Old Mother Goose, When she wanted to wander.* As the fame of the old pantomime dame increased, her sway over nursery rhymes diminished.

But what about *Songs for the Nursery or Mother Goose*? The work which John Fleet Eliot, the great, great grandson of the said Mother Goose swore that his ancestress had written. He swore also that his friend Edward A Crowninshield, aged 24 and a 'literary gentleman', had seen copies of a mutilated version of the 1719 edition in the library of the American Antiquarian Society in Worcester, Massachusetts in 1843. "Unhappily," or as Peter and Iona Opie (the great experts on nursery rhymes) went on to point out "perhaps happily for the fable, Crowninshield died eleven months before Eliot brought himself to refer to the discovery".

Thomas Fleet's 'great work' never came to light. Soon after John Fleet Eliot mentioned it in 1860 antiquarians scoured the records and the shelves of the Library of the Antiquarian Society in Worcester. No trace was found. They rifled through records and shelves of Benjamin Franklin's Library in Philadelphia to see if there was any record of it, because this library was reputed to have a copy of every book published in the colonies. Not a trace. Perhaps it would have come to the attention of Isaiah Thomas, one of the greatest book collectors of all time. He was the grandson of Thomas Fleet, the great grandson of the supposed authoress, and would almost certainly have published her verses had they ever seen the light of day. But no copy was found in his collection either.

Unless further evidence pops up, the existence of these Mother Goose *'Songs'* must be extremely doubtful. This wasn't the first and it wasn't the last of the *'fabuleux et faux'* to be associated with Mother Goose.

Suspect grave! Legendary goose-footed Queen Bertha! Doubtful publication sunk without trace! Welcome again to *The Mother Goose Mysteries*!

Tim Devlin
July 28th 2024

NOTES FOR READERS

In the foreword to my last book *Cracking Humpty Dumpty* I describe how Mary Cooper, an enterprising bookseller, had the marvellous idea of collecting and publicising old rhymes often found on scraps of paper or lodged in people's memories. They were published under the title of *Tommy Thumb's Pretty Song book* in 1744. The second volume in the British Library is the oldest existing collection of nursery rhymes but then they weren't called as such – just "rhymes", or "little jingles".

Twenty or so years earlier Ambrose Philips, a staunch Whig and writer of pastoral poems, used to send rhyming jingles to the children of his sponsors and supporters. He was much mocked by the poet Alexander Pope and others. Another poet and satirist, Henry Carey, penned a savage critique of Philips's work in 1725 when he wrote *Namby Pamby: A Panegyric on the New Versification*. The title suggests that childish jingles were in those days becoming a new genre at least in well-to-do nurseries. His cruellest lines (and coarsest) are as follows:

> *Namby-Pamby's little rhymes*
> *Little jingles, little chimes*
> *To repeat to missy-miss,*
> *Piddling ponds of pissy-piss;*

And a little later:

> *Now he pumps his little wits*
> *Shitting writes, and writing shits,*
> *All by tiny little bits.*
> *And methinks I hear him say*
> *Boys and girls come out to play!*

Unwittingly *Namby Pamby* has turned out to be an invaluable first reference to this odd bunch of ballads, short pieces of satirical writing known as 'squibs', and jingly rhymes. Three rhymes in this book are mentioned in this skittish poem: *Little Jack Horner*, *London Bridge* and *Ride a Cock Horse*.

The term 'nursery rhyme' was not used until the beginning of the 19th century and it did not become an established term until the 1840s. A Shakespearean scholar, James Orchard Halliwell, placed as many jingles as he could find into a series of nursery rhyme collections called *The Nursery Rhymes of England* which was first published in 1842.

By then the idea that some of these jingles might refer to human beings or specific events had been put forward by an eccentric botanist called John Bellenden Ker in a weird essay on the archaeology of nursery rhymes first published in 1837. His bizarre work, however, made a deep impression on an American sleuth called Katherine Elwes Thomas who in 1930 wrote *The Real Personages of Mother Goose*. Ever since then several detectives including me have been trying to link nursery rhymes to historical figures.

After my first book - *Cracking Humpty Dumpty* - was published at the end of 2022 a learned academic described what I had written as 'historiography'. This involves looking at historical sources and in this case rumours about nursery rhymes to see how valid they are. Each rhyme in both books has been chosen because someone has suggested in print that it could be about a historical event or person.

I have used *The Oxford Dictionary of Nursery Rhymes* by the remarkable Peter and Iona Opie to trace the earliest surviving version of each rhyme. They are mentioned so many times in this book that I have referred to them simply as 'the Opies'. They suggested many clues to their origin sometimes in such small print that it is no wonder that few other people knew about them. They were too academic to make firm suggestions about the origin and meaning of these rhymes except for one rhyme mentioned in this book: *London Bridge is falling down* (Chapter 7). They were sure it was about human sacrifice!

Otherwise they leave it to folklorists, collectors of nursery rhymes and writers and former journalists like me to come up with suggestions. As Lady Maxse recommended (see the first page of both books) I have pooled together the wisdom (and often wit) of those mentioned on the next page. My aim is to record for posterity as many theories as possible about these rhymes before they are forgotten and then suggest the one that to me seems the most likely.

In my final chapter I make a plea for the future survival of the nursery rhyme itself in an age when children are brought up on technological gadgets and cell-phones rather than nursery rhymes.

MAIN WORKS CONSULTED

Date	Author	Title	Publisher
1837	John Bellenden Ker	An Essay on the Archæology of Our Popular Phrases and Nursery Rhymes	Longman, Rees, Orme, Brown, Green & Co and Coupland, Southampton
1842	James Orchard Halliwell	The Nursery Rhymes of England	Percy Society
1892	G.F. Northall	English Folk Rhymes	Kegan Paul, Trench, Trübner & Co.
1897	Andrew Lang	The Nursery Rhyme Book	Frederick Warne and Co.
1899	Percy B Green	A History of Nursery Rhymes	Greening and Co.
1906	Lina Eckenstein	Comparative Studies in Nursery Rhymes	Duckworth & Co.
1919	Elmer Boyd Smith	The Boyd Smith Mother Goose	G.P. Putnam's Sons
1924	Henry Bett	Nursery Rhymes and Tales	Methuen & Co.
1930	Katherine Elwes Thomas	The Real Personages of Mother Goose	Lothrop, Lee & Shepard Co.
1947	Lewis Spence	Myth and Ritual in Dance, Game and Rhyme	Watts & Co.
1951	Iona & Peter Opie	The Oxford Dictionary of Nursery Rhymes	Oxford University Press
1956	Professor David Daube	The Oxford Magazine	The Oxonian
1962	William & Ceil Baring-Gould	The Annotated Mother Goose	Clarkson N, Potter Inc.
1968	Albert Mason Stevens	The Nursery Rhyme: Remnant of Popular Protest	Coronado Press
1977	Jean Harrowven	Origins of Rhymes, Songs and Sayings	Kaye & Ward
1985	Iona & Peter Opie	The Singing Game	Oxford University Press
1986	Norman Iles	Who Really Killed Cock Robin?	Robert Hale
1987	Gloria T Delamar	Mother Goose From Nursery to Literature	McFarland
2003	Chris Roberts	Heavy Words Lightly Thrown	Granta Books

MAIN WORKS CONSULTED | 15

Date	Author	Title	Publisher
2008	Albert Jack	*Pop Goes the Weasel*	Allen Lane
2010	Colin Bullock	*Notes on the entymology of Nursery Rhymes*	Frittenden Parish Magazine
2013	Linda Alchin	*The Secret History of Nursery Rhymes*	www.rhymes.org.uk
2017	Oliver Tearle	*The Best Nursery Rhymes Everyone Should Know*	Interestingliterature.com
2018	Diana Ferguson	*Ring A Ring O'Roses*	Michael O'Mara Books Limited
2018	Sandy Leong	*Warts & All*	Amazon

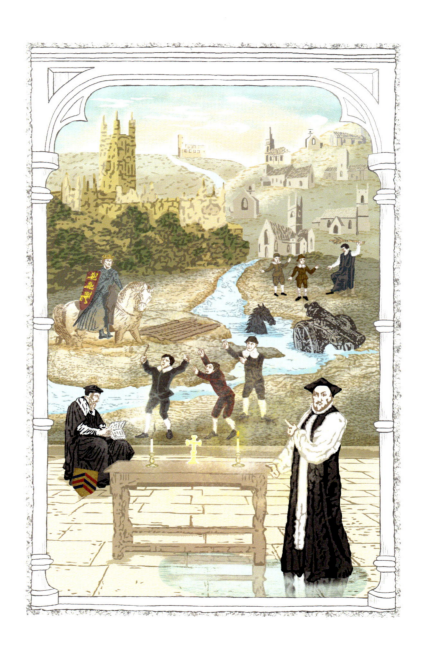

CHAPTER ONE

DOCTOR FOSTER

When the inspector didn't call.

Doctor Foster went to Gloucester
In a shower of rain;
He stepped in a puddle,
Right up to his middle,
And never went there again.

My search for Dr Foster led me to an ancient and remote country church in Gloucestershire, the only one in the country where the communion table is still some way down the aisle. Next door in an adjoining old farmhouse I had a cup of tea with some of its parishioners and discussed the reliability of a Scottish cleric who had his own theory about the origin of Dr Foster and where and when he stepped into the puddle.

Who was Dr Foster? Did he ever exist, or could this be just a cautionary rhyme for toddlers warning them to be very careful before stepping into puddles? In some versions of the rhyme the doctor stepped into a 'piddle' (to rhyme with 'middle'). The Opies, the great nursery rhyme collectors, said in their *Oxford Dictionary of Nursery Rhymes* (1951) that it had "little traceable history".

The oldest surviving version of the rhyme appeared in James Orchard Halliwell's 1844 collection of nursery rhymes with no explanation as to its origin. The earliest theory I could find linked the good doctor to royalty. In 1920 Elmer Boyd Smith, one of the writers mentioned in my foreword, suggested that it might refer to a time before streets were paved and when the roads in Gloucester were particularly poor. He wrote: "There is a story told about Edward I riding through the street one night on horseback and being stuck in the mud so deep that it was necessary to place boards on the ground before they were able to carry him into the tavern. He never returned to the place again. It may be that this rhyme refers to him."

This is the story behind the rhyme which is generally accepted if you surf the internet for its origins. But Mr Boyd Smith's use of the word 'maybe' suggests a lack of certainty although many interpreters of nursery rhymes have taken his guess for gospel.

Edward I was very tall by modern standards let alone in the second half of the 13th century: 6 feet 2 inches. Hence his well-known nickname: 'Longshanks.' Would someone as tall as that have been worried about a ditch, however deep? And as for a puddle or piddle? Neither seem very threatening to a man of his stature.

He went to Gloucester at least three times. As Prince Edward he led the force which managed to break into Gloucester Castle to relieve the garrisons during the civil war in 1263. A year later he was captured by Simon de Montfort, leader of the revolting barons, and imprisoned in the castle. He escaped – so didn't get stuck in a puddle. But he probably *did* go 'there again'. This was in 1278 when he was king. He held a parliament there which passed the Statutes of Gloucester. Again no mention of a puddle. Edward I wasn't a doctor and he wasn't nicknamed Dr Foster.

Dr William Chillingworth was a doctor, an army chaplain and a military expert in the Civil War between Cavaliers and Roundheads during which Charles I tried unsuccessfully to put Gloucester under siege in 1643. According to Professor David Daube, another of my nursery rhyme detectives and a distinguished Professor of Law at Oxford University, Dr Chillingworth could have been Dr Foster. He outlined this theory in a series of articles about the origin of nursery rhymes for the *Oxford Magazine* in 1956.

He credited Chillingworth with being the inventor of Humpty Dumpty, the siege engine, built like a giant tortoise, which collapsed in the river at Gloucester in 1643 (see my last book: *Cracking Humpty Dumpty*). The professor wondered: "whether another rhyme does not concern the same incident. May Dr Chillingworth not be the 'Dr Foster' who went to Gloucester? His own name would not be suitable for a rhyme. The next best thing would be to take a name that rhymed with 'Gloucester'. The poem must refer to a well-known scholar: the Doctor title was not then so easily got as nowadays. The scholar in question must have suffered a humiliating experience at Gloucester. And the details are highly reminiscent of what happened to the learned constructor of the 'tortoise'. It was the wet moat the 'puddle' into which he unfortunately 'stepped right up to his middle' which proved his undoing. Certainly 'he never went there again'. The royal army left never to return and Dr Chillingworth himself died in January 1644."

This theory like Humpty Dumpty the trundling tortoise-shaped cannon was another spoof put forward by the imaginative Dr Daube who was fond of jokes and riddles. According to the *National Dictionary of Biography*: "it was not always easy to know how seriously to take what he said or wrote".

There is another rhyme about Dr Foster which was discovered nearly 40 years before James Halliwell published his version. It was in the collection of Francis Douce, an antiquarian and one time Keeper of Manuscripts at the British Museum. Dated c1805 it went like this:

> *Dr Foster was a good man,*
> *He whipped his scholars now and then;*
> *When he whipped them he made them dance*
> *Out of England into France.*

This rhyme also appeared in James Orchard Halliwell's first collection of nursery rhymes in 1842. Here the 'good man' was called 'Dr Faustus', with a note saying 'perhaps Foster'. This has led to speculation that Dr Foster was the Dr Faustus who sold his soul to the devil in the Faustian legend. In the play by Christopher Marlowe published in 1604 there is a reference to a 'horse courser' paying Doctor Faustus forty dollars and riding his horse into a deep pond and nearly drowning when the horse suddenly vanishes. But there is no connection between Dr Faustus and Gloucester in the Marlowe tragedy so I searched for another possible connection with the city.

Katherine Elwes Thomas, who wrote *The Real Personages of Mother Goose* (1930) provided a possible link. An American, she was one of the first people to connect nursery rhymes to historical incidents. She had Dr Faustus going to Gloucester when it was under siege in the Civil War in a shower of rain or "bullets from the Roundheads".

The Royalists found themselves in a 'puddle up to their middle' and 'Dr Fauster' – a hybrid of the two – was most woefully bespattered with mud either at Gloucester or at a later battle at Newberry (Newbury). As with most of Thomas's theories I didn't believe this one. Writing about her recently, Robert Waltz, the editor of the *Traditional Ballad Index,* commented: "We should note, though, that Thomas could connect with anything except reality!"

Another rhyme about a third Dr Foster appeared in an edition of nursery rhymes collected by an antiquarian called Joseph Ritson. *Gammer Gurton's Garland* was published in 1810 - 34 years before the Dr Foster puddle rhyme. Headed with the title 'The Sedate Preacher' it went like this:

> *Old Dr. Forster*
> *Went to Glo'ster,*
> *To preach the word of God:*
> *When he came there,*
> *He sate in his chair,*
> *And gave all the people a nod.*

But is he the same person as the Doctor Foster who went to Gloucester in a shower of rain? Halliwell in his 1844 collection of rhymes probably thought so. He put the two rhymes one after another with a picture of a rather fat priggish preacher in-between. So I have combined them and have concentrated on the line about giving all the people 'a nod'.

Assuming that this Dr Foster was a Doctor of Divinity, my trail started with finding a famous clergyman who had strong connections with Gloucester. This put me on to William Laud, born in 1573, a student at St John's College, Oxford, who earned his doctorate in 1608. He was a High Church Anglican who was appointed Dean of Gloucester in 1616 by King James I on a mission to clean up the cathedral.

The Gloucester Cathedral Chapter Act Book (1616-1687) recorded his attempts to put things right. The cathedral was in a poor state. According to Suzanne Eward, who in 2019 edited the *Chapter Act Book*, King James had warned Laud that there "was scarce a Church in England so ill govern'd and so much out of order". An earlier report by the Calvinist Bishop Miles Smith mentioned a canon there, one William Loe, who was suspected of adultery with his servant who had become pregnant. Gardens had been sacrilegiously laid out over sacred burial grounds. Two people were said to be selling 'drink within the premises' and the choristers were running riot because there was no one there to 'catechise them'. But worst of all when Dr Laud arrived he found that the wooden communion table had been taken from its rightful place by the altar and was halfway down the 45 metre 'quire' (long aisle with choir stalls) where it had been placed east to west rather than 'altarwise' – north to south.

When I visited the cathedral on a cold winter's morning in February 2023 Rebecca Phillips, the cathedral's archivist, placed the original 17th century chapter book on a white cushion and laid it on a table at the end of the long library. With her help, I read the passage dated 27th January 1616 (without the brackets which have been put in a translation for a better understanding): "It was by Mr deane and the chapter aforesaid ordered and decreed that the communion table should be place(d) altar wise at the upper ende of the quier close und(er the) walle upon the uppermost greeses or steppes acc(ording) as it is used in the king's majestie's chappell and in (all) or the moste parte of the cathedral churches of (the) realme."

Later entries refer to the ruinous fabric and great decay of the cathedral but Dr Laud was most concerned about the position of the communion table. High Anglicans regarded the communion service as a special sacrament. To them, as Susanne Eward explains, communion was a sacrament and the taking of it was a 'climax' to the liturgy. It had to be properly taken at the altar, facing north-south at the top of the cathedral. To the Puritans the communion table, was just that, a wooden table to be used much more informally for a commemorative meal.

When Laud insisted that all the canons, choirmen, choristers and the under officers should bow humbly to Almighty God when they approached the table it caused an uproar. Suzanne Eward wrote: "The Calvinist bishop Miles Smith disliked bowing and ceremonial in worship and strongly protested at what had been done. Almost the whole population of puritan Gloucester was offended at the moving of the communion table, and a libellous paper was placed in the pulpit of St Michael's church accusing the canons of not having spirit enough to resist the dean……"

David Verey and David Welander in their history of *Gloucester Cathedral* (1989) described how Dr Laud placed stout altar rails made of oak (part of which can now be seen in the Lady Chapel) "so as to prevent dogs fouling the sanctuary". They reported how Bishop Miles Smith said he would never set foot in the Cathedral again." That might have fitted in with the "never went there again" of the puddle rhyme. But tempers were cooled by the efforts of an alderman called John Jones and in 1624 Bishop Smith did go into the cathedral again. He was buried there beneath a plain marble slab! His two daughters both died in childbirth and predeceased him in 1622 and 1623. They have monuments to their names in the Lady Chapel. So presumably he attended their funerals.

William Prynne, a leading Puritan pamphleteer of the time, was one of the prosecutors of Archbishop Laud (as he later became) during his trial for treason in 1644. The making of 'low obeyance to it (Gloucester communion table) as if Christ were there upon it" was used in evidence against Laud. Prynne wrote in *Canterburies Doome* "how much thereby the secret Papist would be stirred up to rejoice…."

This was hardly the reaction I had expected from the nursery rhyme where, as I recorded earlier in this chapter, the sedate preacher "sat in his chair and gave all the people a nod". I eliminated Laud and Smith from my search but not entirely. Laud left Gloucester in 1621 to become Bishop of St David's in Wales. But more than 10 years later he was appointed Archbishop of Canterbury by Charles I in 1633.

William Holden Hutton, whose biography of Laud was published in 1893, wrote: "Established at Canterbury with the full support of the King, Laud determined upon a great effort to make the English Church recognize and display its unity through an uniformity of worship and ceremonial, which its formularies undoubtedly contemplated, and which only the leading influence of foreign Protestantism had disturbed. Accordingly in 1634 he instituted a visitation of all the dioceses of his province."

The man he appointed to carry out this task was Dr Brent, a doctor of Common Law from Oxford University. He was now also Sir Nathaniel Brent, Warden of Merton College, Oxford, and had the title of Vicar General to the Archbishop. He was well-connected having married the niece of the previous archbishop of Canterbury. He was born around 1573 so would have been into his sixties at the time of the proposed visitation. Old enough to be called 'old'.

An article in *Gloucestershire History No 8 (February 1994)* by Philip Brown claimed that Dr Brent was Dr Foster. He arrived in Gloucester for a two-day visit on June 8th and 9th 1635 and in a report to Laud which was recorded in the preface to the *Calendar of State Papers (Domestic)* of that year: "Here was much solemnity, many orations and great entertainment. In the Cathedral Church many things amiss. No cope; the fabric in decay; an annuity of £201 per annum given by one Mr Cox is scarce well-bestowed. The Schoolmaster refused to take the oath. I suspended him but decreed the execution thereof should be stayed until they heard from me again."

Dr Brent also railed against the extravagance of the cathedral employing "cookes, butlers and others" and decreed that their stipends should end "when theire places shal become voyd". His visitation was mentioned in the cathedral's *Chapter Act Book* over a year later in November 1636.

Clearly Dr Brent was not going out of his way to make friends and his orders were probably much mocked. It might have been dangerous to refer to the archbishop's chosen representative by name so a pseudonym was used which rhymed with Gloucester. It provided a picture, said Philip Brown, of a rather superior figure 'who gave all the people a nod' and came to lay down laws and regulations where none were wanted.

I think this is the best explanation that we have so far for the identity of 'Old Doctor Foster'. The historian Hugh Trevor-Roper could have been describing the reaction to Dr Foster when he described how people at the time reacted with a nod to Dr Brent. In his biography of Archbishop Laud (1940) he wrote: "Brent's visitation was like a passing wind and no more…..Wherever Brent went, he received entertainment, respect and apparent obedience, from local authorities, clergy and gentry: but on his departure, all reverted to their old ways….."

But what about the puddle? Can it be identified? No weather records were kept by the city in 1635 but Gloucester can become very flooded in summer as on July 20 2007 when according to the *Gloucester News* 78mm of rain fell on the city causing rapid and intense flash flooding stranding some 500 people at the railway station. So the old Dr Foster rhyme might have been used in a jingle about the flood-hit city. Could there have been a particular incident when the old cleric stepped into a puddle?

A "crucial first clue" was given to Philip Brown, the man who linked Dr Foster to Nathaniel Brent, by Janet Wilton, a local historian, which I followed up. Her daughter was a member of a school party which in the early 1960s visited the ancient Anglo-Saxon church of St Mary's Priory whose origins date back to the early 9th century. This is in Deerhurst a village some nine miles north of Gloucester on the east bank of the river Severn. The road to it is often flooded and was so in the 17th century.

The vicar at the time of the school outing was a Scot, the Reverend Hugh Maclean, who had been appointed in 1938 and died in 1981. He told the school party that Doctor Foster had been an emissary of William Laud and had visited Gloucester with instructions that all communion tables should be placed at the east end of the church and removed from the chancel if they were there. But he had not been able to reach Deerhurst, where the communion table is in the chancel, because the Severn was in flood.

The interesting thing about St Mary's Priory Church is that its communion table is still in the chancel and with seats all around it. Arthur Mee, author of *The King's England, Gloucestershire* (1966), described it as "a sort of village sanctuary" and believed this arrangement to be "remarkable for something we have not come across elsewhere".

The stalls contain seats around the east end of the chancel behind the communion table, a practice which was not uncommon in churches after Queen Elizabeth came to the throne, but denounced by Laud, when he was Bishop of London, when he told churchwardens: "You must not prepare your seates above God."

Philip Brown listed a number of city and rural parishes where representatives, vicars, curates, and rectors had been summoned to a meeting in Gloucester and presented with a list of 13 demands which had to be implemented within two months by August 24th. One of them, clause 10, was for the communion table to be set at the upper end of the Chancel north to south. The demands and parishes are listed in the *Gloucester Diocesan Records*. Mr Brown commented: "Deerhurst is **not** among them."

Was it conspicuous by its absence from the records? I checked with both Lambeth Palace (home of the Archbishop of Canterbury) and Merton College, Oxford, the employer of Dr Brent. Neither had any records of Brent visiting Deerhurst.

I contacted Michael Hare who has spent the last 30 years studying the history of St Mary's Priory and has lectured on the chancel and its furnishings. He had not come across the connection between the church and the nursery rhyme before. He sent a copy of Philip Brown's article to Trevor Cooper, a Sussex expert on church furnishings, who was completing a work on *The Post-Reformation Furnishings at St Mary's* which covers the period of Brent's visitation to Gloucester and describes the chancel stalls as "unique and of national importance".

Mr Cooper hadn't heard of the connection with Dr Foster either and pointed out that the diocesan records were not complete. He told me: "Those surviving for Brent's visit only include some of the deaneries – administrative clusters of parishes – in the diocese. Deerhurst belonged to the deanery of Tewkesbury and Winchcombe. Brent's instructions for that deanery do not survive although they were no doubt identical to those for other deaneries. However the absence of Deerhurst in the diocesan records that survive provides no support at all for identifying the nursery rhyme with a failed visit to Deerhurst by Brent."

Cooper's study gives several insights into how the chancel seating and the position of the communion table could have survived the Laudian reforms of the 1630s. He describes Deerhurst at that time as a large agricultural parish in the vale of Gloucester with about 200 communicants (aged over 16) "where Puritan non-conformity was epidemic".

In August 1633 a child was baptised at Deerhurst without the sign of the cross. The offending freelance curate was summoned to Court. The next year the same thing happened to his successor the Reverend Robert Huntington when he disdained to wear a surplice during the service. Clearly the Deerhurst churchwardens refused to remove the seating at the east end of the church when told to do so in 1634. The churchwardens seem to have been happy to allow the men in their congregation to wear hats in church although this was banned in 1604. In November 1639 the churchwardens refused to "tell the names of those that put on theire hats all sermon tyme & prayers". The deliberate wearing of hats in church was often non-conformist virtue signalling. It seems clear that the Priory's chancel fittings did not need the intervention of a flood to help their survival!

Even so could Dr Foster have been the inspector who didn't call? Hugh Maclean, the vicar who had started the rumour, had been dead for more than 40 years. But there were people in the village who knew and remembered him. Michael Hare, who had met him briefly, drove me from Gloucester along the winding lower road, some of it alongside the River Severn where it was easy to see how even a moderate rainfall would make the road treacherous. But the greatest surprise was when we got to the actual church. It's quite frankly in the middle of nowhere, in a tiny village with fewer than 100 inhabitants, filled with beautiful old timber-framed houses.

Purchases in the church warden's accounts of bread and wine suggest that in the 17th century communion services were only held on four feast days a year – Christmas, Easter, Whitsun and Michaelmas. On these occasions, Mr Hare said, the congregation would sit in the nave and would move into the chancel for the communion service only after the final prayer for the church militant had been read out. A picture in the church guidebook shows the table on a red carpet facing west to east in the centre of the chancel as it would have under the Puritan arrangements.

The chancel is magnificently enclosed with fine oak rails and boxed-in pews. Trevor Cooper dated the stalls to probably the early 17th century. He described them in his booklet: "They are of high-quality oak, quarter cut or hewn, with fine medullary rays especially in the flat panels; the carving is excellent; and care has been taken on details such as mouldings."

Changing the position of the table in the chancel would have been an easy job for the churchwardens if they had been so inclined though removing the seating from against the east wall and railing the table in, as was also required, would have taken more effort. To place it by the altar at the top of the church, as in most churches, would have required a major re-structure. The beautiful seven-sided apse which had contained the high altar behind it was destroyed at the Dissolution of the Monasteries (1536-1541). The wall at the top of the chancel was bricked up soon after the dissolution. Mr Hare told me: "There were pigsties in the apse from the 1740s to the 1840s to the distress of those with High Anglican Tractarian tendencies in the 19th Century."

In the 14th century stone farmhouse curiously linked to the church I joined its owner Will Morris and a group of parishioners who remembered Hugh Maclean, none more so than Jean Leeke, a former teacher, and her husband Brian. They spoke of him with affection and said he could be counted on for a number of things as well as shortening his sermons so he and members of his congregation could watch the *Forsyte Saga*, a popular tv programme.

Jean said: "He always visited parishioners in hospital on a Thursday which meant that he could visit the library nearby and claim petrol expenses." He collected jetsam and driftwood from the river to save on firewood and popped in to see parishioners between 6pm and 8pm at a time of day when they might be serving drinks. But as for being a fount of reliable authority the Leakes and their friends all agreed: he would never "let the truth get in the way of a good story".

The flood which prevented Dr Brent's team from reaching Deerhurst in June 1635 was almost certainly a figment of his fertile imagination.

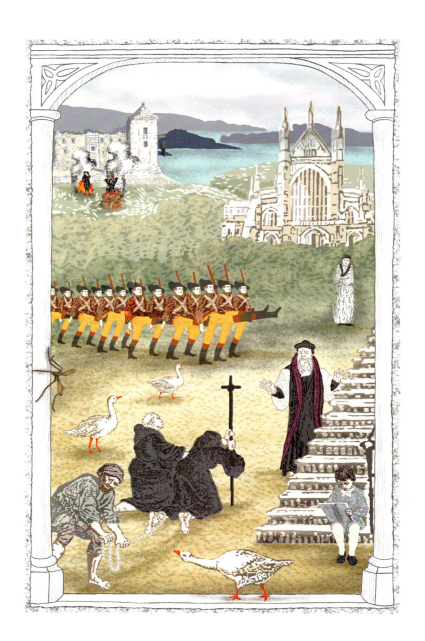

CHAPTER TWO
GOOSEY, GOOSEY, GANDER
The turbulent priest

Goosey, goosey, gander!
Where shall I wander?
Up stairs and down stairs
And in my lady's chamber.

. . . .

There I met an old man,
That would not say his prayers;
I took him by the left leg,
And threw him down the stairs.

There is a mystery about this rhyme: is it one nursery rhyme or two divided by the dotted line above? The first rhyme is about a roving gander and the second about an obstinate old man.

A Dictionary of English Folklore by Jacqueline Simpson and Steve Roud (2000) explained: "Historically speaking the rhyme seems to have less textual cohesion than most nursery rhymes, and there is evidence that this standard modern text is actually two older rhymes spliced together. The first four lines are quoted in c1784, and first printed c.1790, while the last four of a similar age but are often found in a traditional rhyme addressed to the cranefly."

The earliest surviving version of the first verse appeared in Joseph Ritson's *Gammer Gurton's Garland* as follows:

> *GOOSE-a, goose-a, gander,*
> *Where shall I wander?*
> *Up stairs, down stairs,*
> *In my lady's chamber;*
> *There you'll find a cup of sack,*
> *And a race of ginger.*

The Opies pointed out that this version didn't embrace the last four lines and it was "very probable that they had a separate origin". The last four lines were much the same as those cruel schoolchildren addressed to a cranefly (or daddy long legs), while sometimes pulling off its legs. *Nancy Cock's Song Book* which was published in 1744 had a rhyme which went:

> *Old father Long-Legs*
> *Can't say his Prayers:*
> *Take him by the Left Leg,*
> *And throw him down Stairs.*

The Opies provided a somewhat bizarre explanation. Writing in 1951 they referred to a child who some 150 years ago added the rhyme to "his or her" nursery rhyme book and amalgamated the two distinct pieces together. Perhaps this was a joke on their part as there is evidence, which they appear not to have seen, that the two verses of the poem were together at least 150 if not more years before the Opies completed their dictionary of nursery rhymes in 1951.

By 1800 the rhyme had in fact been set to music and appeared on page 42 of a copy of Samuel Arnold's *Juvenile Amusements* (1797) which I found in the British Library. This is the oldest surviving collection of nursery rhymes set to music collected by one of the leading figures in London's musical life at that time. However Arnold is not listed by the Opies among the notable figures in their dictionary and there is other evidence to indicate that they may not have seen the Arnold collection. There are a few examples of very early nursery rhymes in it which they appear not to have spotted.

The Goosey Gander rhyme in this 142-page volume, containing 64 nursery rhymes, was more or less in the same form as we have today, incorporating both the goose and the old man (described as "poor") who wouldn't say his prayers and was "kicked down the stairs".

If Arnold's version was not the result of a schoolchild error, why or when did the gander meet the old man? Or could the two be one and the same? And did the all-important clue in line six – "would not say his prayers" suggest that the gander might have been a priest.

'Yes' said Katherine Elwes Thomas in *The Real Personages of Mother Goose* (1930). The old man who wouldn't say his prayers and the goosey gander could have been Cardinal David Beaton, Lord Chancellor of Scotland. He was killed in a Protestant-led conspiracy on 29th May 1546 at his home, St Andrews Castle in Fife. He was thrown down the stairs by the Protestant Covenanters, stabbed to death and his naked bleeding body was then hung from the castle's ramparts.

Julia Morrison in the magazine *History* ((29/5/2020) wrote about his 'macabre' murder. She didn't link the cardinal to the nursery rhyme. But she did provide a clue as to how he might have been frequenting 'lady's chambers!' She wrote: "Furthermore, he fathered a number of illegitimate children. He had eight children with a woman called Marion Ogilvy. She was his wife in all but name for two decades. It's widely accepted that he also had children outside of this relationship. His conduct in his personal life is perhaps more shocking to a modern audience, but it was likely still frowned upon in his lifetime."

He had many enemies. He spent, according to Julia Morrison, vast sums of the Church's money as if it were his own and indulged in nepotism appointing many members of his own family to high positions in the Church. He would have been regarded by Protestants as the embodiment of what the Reformation was all about – the need to eradicate corrupt practices.

On 1st March 1546 he had the Protestant preacher George Wishart burnt for heresy at the stake in the grounds of his castle home. Wishart was a close friend of the Scottish preacher John Knox. In his *Historie of the Reformation of Religion in Scotland* (1566) Knox was happy to relate what happened in revenge to Beaton's bleeding corpse: 'because the weather was hot…….. it was thought best – to keep him from stinking – to give him great salt enough, a cope of lead, and a nuik (nook) in the bottom of the sea tower…..'. Cardinal Beaton was 51 or possibly 52 when he died 59 days after Wishart. In those days he would have been considered to have been an old man.

Albert Mason Stevens, a little-known rhyme detective and an American Oxford-educated scholar, had another solution. In *The Nursery Rhyme – Remnant of Popular Protest* (1968), published some years after his death, he suggested that the gander was an English Lord Chancellor, Stephen Gardiner. He was a much-hated Bishop of Winchester in the reign of Mary I (Mary Tudor or Bloody Mary). Stevens cited the Puritan satirist Edward Hake as nicknaming him 'Romishe Goose' because of his religion and connection with Winchester.

He could have frequented many a 'lady's chamber' either in gossip or in fact. The Bishop of Winchester, according to Patricia Pierce's book *Old London Bridge* (2002), controlled most of the "immensely profitable" Bankside brothels in Southwark where prostitutes were even nicknamed "Winchester Geese". Furthermore, Stephen Gardiner had a palace in Southwark overlooking the Thames. Pierce reported: "From 1531 Stephen Gardiner appointed a Henry Frances 'Bayliffe of the Clinke and Capteyn of the Stewes [brothels] and all the whores'."

'In my lady's chamber' might also have referred to a scurrilous scandal going around at the time that Gardiner was Queen Mary's lover and she was even thought to be pregnant with his child. This was related by John Strype in his *Memorials of Cranmer* published in 1694. Completely untrue said Stevens but it could still be an important part of the rhyme.

Albert Jack, author of *Pop Goes The Weasel* (2008) believed Goosey Gander was a Roman Catholic recusant priest and the origin of the rhyme dated back to 16th century England and the "Papist purge". The goose after all was a sacred symbol of ancient Rome. Gander is a male goose. Livy describes how their cackling was used as an alarm signal notably in the 4th century AD when the Gauls were approaching the Capitol Hill. The prayer book was in English, Albert Jack wrote, and Catholics refused to use it. A Catholic priest would say his prayers in Latin not English. He was discovered in 'my lady's chamber' – i.e. the bedroom of the mistress of the house where many papist bolt holes were located in walls, chimney rests or underneath floorboards. 'Whither do I wander' referred to the raids by Queen Elizabeth's spies and priest-trackers.

Linda Alchin writing *The Secret History of Nursery Rhymes* five years later agreed with the recusant priest theory and said the rhyme has a moral that something unpleasant would surely happen if you don't say your prayers correctly "meaning the Protestant Prayers, said in English as opposed to Catholic prayers which were said in Latin". You get thrown down the stairs.

And possible suspects? Perhaps the famous Jesuit priest found two months after the notorious Gunpowder Plot in 1605. Eleven priest holes were discovered in Hindlip Hall, the Worcestershire home of the Catholics Thomas and Mary Habington. The search started on 20th January 1606 and lasted 12 days. Four priests were eventually found: Nicholas Owen aged 43 and Ralph Ashley, whose birth date is unknown, but he was probably younger, Father Edward Oldcorne aged 44, and the most likely Goosey, Goosey candidate, Father Henry Garnet aged 60. But Garnet and Oldcorne, frail and famished, gave themselves up after a week, and were not found in a lady's bedchamber.

Much as I would like to find historical characters for nursery rhymes, I'm not sure about the Catholic priest version. When Catholic recusant priests were eventually dragged out of their priest holes they were usually in such a feeble state of undernourishment that the last thing you would do is to throw them down the stairs and pull them up again. That might have killed them. That's not what Sir Richard Topcliffe, the most famous and brutal of them, and all the other leading hunters of Catholic priests wanted. They wanted them alive so that they could be tortured, brought to trial and then hung, drawn and quartered.

Sandy Leong in her book *Warts & All* (2018) dated the poem several years later to the persecution of Catholics by Oliver Cromwell. Goosey, Goosey Gander referred to the goose step march of the Commonwealth militia as they hunted their unfortunate victims down. A common punishment she says was to put a rope round the left leg of priests and then haul them back and ask them to say their prayers in English, the Protestant way. She adds that the term 'left leg' or 'left foot' was still to this day a derogatory term for Catholics in the UK.

This is true but it seems that the term 'left footer' as a derogatory term for Catholics was not introduced until the Troubles in Ireland during the 20th century. According to *Brewer's Dictionary of Phrase & Fable* it could have been a reference to their use of a turf-cutting spade which had to be dug with the left foot!

Katharine Elwes Thomas's theory about Cardinal Beaton would have more weight if the rhyme sounded more Scottish. The rhyme is clearly about two separate entities meeting each other - the roving gander and the obstinate old man. The theory put forward by Dr Stevens brings the two halves of the rhyme neatly together.

It places Stephen Gardiner as the 'Romishe Goose', possible frequenter of brothels, who was scurrilously linked to 'my lady's chamber'. He had his victim burnt at the stake (or thrown down the stairs) on the 21st March 1556. The victim was Thomas Cramner, former Archbishop of Canterbury during the reign of the Protestant Edward VI. But he was deposed and imprisoned by the Catholic Mary I when she came to the throne in 1553. And then put to death. He died an old man aged 65 and there is good evidence he refused to say his prayers in Latin.

The distinguished Church historian Diarmaid MacCulloch in his life of *Thomas Cramner* (1996) described how the archbishop was furious when one of his bishops in 1553 soon after the death of Edward VI said Mass on his behalf in Canterbury Cathedral. Cramner wrote a declaration to show that when Mary Tudor came to the throne and England suddenly reverted to Catholicism, he had not betrayed the Reformation of the previous reign. A little later he was arrested after he denounced the Latin mass as "of the devil's devising". As copies of his declaration spread around the city one evangelical Londoner was reported in a manuscript as saying: "The Bishop of Canterbury is the old man he was" – the old man who wouldn't say his prayers.

CHAPTER THREE

HICKORY, DICKORY, DOCK

Found in translation

Hickory, dickory, dock,
The mouse ran up the clock.
The clock struck one,
The mouse ran down,
Hickory, dickory, dock.

"While Oliver Cromwell has often been described as a lion, his eldest son Richard Cromwell was frequently portrayed as a mouse – the legacy of this former Felsted schoolboy being a nursery rhyme: *Hickory Dickory Dock.*"

So wrote Paul Wreyford in *The A-Z of Curious ESSEX*, an English county guide published in 2013. When he got to 'F' he began his entry on Felsted: "Many former pupils of the famous Felsted School have gone on to achieve great things." But Richard Cromwell was not one of them. He became a figure of fun, mocked and taunted by his enemies shortly after he succeeded his father as Protector of the Commonwealth of England in 1658. Lacking sufficient military experience to rule an army-controlled state, he succumbed and two years later the monarchy was restored under Charles II.

Paul Wreyford wrote: "The rhyme *Hickory Dickory Dock* is reputedly a reference to his short reign. Richard is the mouse that returns from where it came from when the clock strikes one – symbolising a year in power, though he did not quite even reign for that long – just nine months or so."

Albert Jack wrote that the rhyme "is believed by some to have been inspired by the last man ever to rule England as a republic". Sandy Leong in *Warts & All* (2018) claimed that Richard Cromwell had several nicknames "because he was seen as an ineffectual leader. He was called Queen Dick, Tumbledown Dick and Hickory Dick".

In 1972 Professor Earl Malcolm Hause, of the University of Idaho, wrote a book entitled: *Tumbledown Dick: the fall of the House of Cromwell*. In it he quoted the reactions of a member of an old Buckinghamshire family recorded 200 years after Richard's abdication on 25th May 1659 by their descendant Frances Parthenope Verney: "So easy is it to fall. Honest, kind-hearted and conscientious, but he was hopelessly discredited as a ruler, this mute inglorious Cromwell, guiltless of his country's blood, retired into complete obscurity with 'a comfortable and honourable subsistence,' and with the people's nickname of 'Tumble-down Dick'."

Although Mr Cromwell lived on in obscurity under the pseudonym 'John Clarke' until he was 85, there was nothing in these family memoirs or in Professor Hause's book to show that he was also called 'Hickory Dick' and that this nickname wasn't a posthumous one bestowed on him unkindly after the rhyme was published.

It's one of our oldest surviving rhymes. It appeared in Volume II of *Tommy Thumb's Pretty Song Book* (c1744) where it began:

> *Hickere, Dickere Dock*
> *A Mouse ran up the Clock,*
> *The Clock Struck One,*
> *The Mouse fell down,*
> *And Hickere Dickere Dock.*

But who was the mouse if not Richard Cromwell? About 20 years later the rhyme cropped up again in *Mother Goose's Melody or Sonnets for the Cradle* written in about 1765 and published in England around 1780. It began 'DICKERY, Dickery Dock' and was accompanied by a woodcut of a grandfather clock with an octagonal face. The maxim in a footnote beneath it read: "Time stands for no man." The rhyme is quite clearly about time and the clock could be a clue.

On the inside wall of the north tower of Exeter Cathedral there is a clock built by a Glastonbury monk displaying the day of the lunar month and the phase of the moon as well as the time. This astronomical clock was built in the late 15th century according to the distinguished art historian Nikolaus Pevsner. It has the inscription *'pereunt et imputantur'* - they perish and are accounted for – which was borrowed from the *Epigrams* of the Roman poet Martial and, in this context, could refer to the passing of the hours.

The clock-room is behind the dial on the north transept wall which still houses the clock mechanism. Access is via a doorway visible in the stone wall directly beneath the clock. At the bottom of the wooden door there is a round hole made in the 17th century to enable a cat to enter the clock and chase the rats and other vermin attracted by the animal fat which was used in medieval times to grease the clock's ropes and cords.

Paul Greaves, a court reporter for the *Devon News*, wrote an article 27/9/2020 which claimed that the crucial link between the clock and the rhyme could be traced to a cat owned by William Cotton, who was Bishop of Exeter from 1598 until his death in 1621. Greaves wrote: "It is from this time that we have the record: 'Paid ye carpenters 8d for cutting ye hole in ye north transept door for ye Bishop's cat'!"

Richard Surman, author of *Cathedral Cats* (2005) was not so sure. "Whether the nursery rhyme Hickory Dickory Dock really did have its origins at Exeter Cathedral is disputable" but he went on: "medieval archives show that there was a cat on the cathedral staff, who received a weekly payment of one penny".

In July 2022 the cathedral shop in the north transept was selling two cathedral guidebooks both with a picture of a cat peeping out of the hole. It was operating a few yards away from the hole where a black knitted cat, with white stripes in its tail, had been strategically placed with its head burrowed inside the clock's door. While the smaller brochure mentions that the clock is "thought to have been the origin of the nursery rhyme", the larger book *Exeter Cathedral: The Garden of Paradise* (2020) by Dr Jonathan Fowle with Diane Walker makes no mention of Hickory Dickory Dock. Evidently they could find no proof to suggest that the clock had any connection with a rhyme.

Evidence that *Hickory Dickory Dock* is about the passage of time mounted up as successive collections of nursery rhymes were published and included it as a counting rhyme. As early as August 1821 the rhyme was being talked about as being part of a favourite children's game. It was mentioned in *Blackwood's Magazine*, the well-known Edinburgh literary journal full of miscellany, by a writer with the pseudonym of Christopher Columbus Esquire. Chapter VIII of the 10th volume part II started with a version which went as follows:

Zickety, dickety, dock,
The mouse ran up the nock;
The nock struck one,
Down the mouse ran,
Zickety, dickety, dock .

'Columbus' wrote: "The rhymes used by children to decide who is to begin a game, are much the same…… The one at the head of this chapter is most frequently used for this purpose." He included it among "the chief of those games which were, and still are, the amusement of the children of Edinburgh." Why the word 'nock' was used instead of clock is a mystery as it's a Scottish word for 'notch' or to fit an arrow on a bow.

James Orchard Halliwell in his first collection of rhymes (1842) placed Hickory Dickory in his section on games. He wrote in a short introduction to it: "Children stand round, and are counted one by one by means of this rhyme….. The child upon whom the last number falls is *out* ." He maintained the last line of Hickory Dickory Dock went: 'O' (7), 'U' (8) and 'T' (9) spells 'OUT'!

In 1892 G.F. Northall's rhyme collection (*English Folk Rhymes*) listed 'Hickory (1), Dickory (2) and Dock (3)' among his counting-out rhymes. The 'clock' was (4), 'struck one' was (5), 'the mouse was gone' (6) and he confirmed (7-9) spelt 'OUT'. Along with 'Hickery, hoary, hairy Ann' it was an old Warwickshire rhyme. Andrew Lang in *The Nursery Rhyme Book* (1897) wrote: "Hickory Dickory Dock is a rhyme for counting out a lot of children. The child on whom the last word falls has to run after the others in the game of 'Tig' or 'Chevy'."

Two years later Percy B. Green, writing in *A History of Nursery Rhymes* (1899), talked about the game of hopscotch being played in every village and town of the British Isles. The rhymes used by street children to decide who is to begin a game are numerous and he mentioned the Edinburgh version quoted above. But what do the words Hickory Dickory Dock actually mean and how can we relate them to a counting game?

Linda Alchin did her best when she included it in her *The Secret History of Nursery Rhymes* (2013). She found the word 'Pohickory' in a dictionary of Virginian trees published in 1653. And she also found that the dock leaf we use against nettle stings came from the Latin word *Rumex crispus.* She pointed out that: "Hickory is derived from the North American Indian word Pawcohiccora which is an oily milk-like liquid that is pressed from pounded hickory nuts." But these words have nothing to do with numbers.

The Opies also scoured the language books and found in translation the best solution so far to the origin of hickory dickory dock. They found a dictionary of the Cumbric language containing numbers used by shepherds in Westmoreland. In the *Oxford Companion to the English Language* (1992) 'Cumbric' is described as an old Celtic language like Welsh spoken in the north of Britain until early medieval times. In Borrowdale, an old valley in the Lake District near Keswick, shepherd men used to count their flocks, women would count their knitting stitches, and children would count in games, starting from one to ten as follows:

Yan, tyan, tehera, methera,
Pimp, sethera, lethera,
Hevera, devera, dick

Is that the nearest we can get to Hickere, dickere, dock? If so, the forerunner of the mouse in the rhyme was probably an ambling sheep!

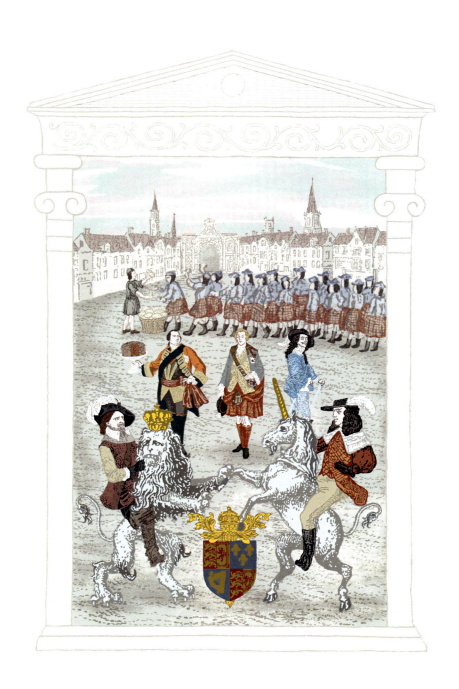

CHAPTER FOUR

LION AND THE UNICORN

The proof of the pudding

The lion and the unicorn
Were fighting for the crown;
The lion beat the unicorn
All round about the town.

Some gave them white bread,
And some gave them brown;
Some gave them plum cake
And drummed them out of town.

And when he had beat him out,
He beat him in again;
He beat him three times over,
His power to maintain.

Was the lion, the king of beasts, a real king in this famous nursery rhyme? And who was the unicorn? Is 'plum-cake' a clue where the date of the pudding could help to identify the famous battle as this delicacy was introduced to England in the mid-17th or early 18th century. And which town is the subject of the rhyme? All will be revealed.

Let's start with the enmity between the lion and the unicorn. It could be at least 2,650 years old or older. The Opies referred to the possibility of these two creatures fighting in the seventh century BC. They said the duel was depicted on a coin minted in the old northern Greek state of Akanthos which was founded around 650BC. They also alluded to an earlier age-old myth that the unicorn, the white horse of spring, each year gave way to the lion, the heat of summer, and that their struggle was mentioned in the earliest English natural history books.

In 2002 Dr Laura Gibbs, a writer and teacher of mythology and folklore at the University of Oklahoma, included *Leo et Unicornis* in a new translation of *Aesop's Fables*. She said it was a very, very, obscure fable in the collection belonging to John Sheppey, a 14th century bishop of Rochester. In it the lion pretended to be lame and went limping up to his chief enemy, the unicorn, to ask if he could borrow his horn as a walking stick so he could visit his sick mother. The unicorn agreed. Without his horn, he was defenceless, so the lion beat him up and wounded him seriously.

Edmund Spenser in the second book of *The Faerie Queen* published in 1590 referred to these contenders when describing a quarrel between two Arthurian knights:

> *Like as a Lyon, whose imperiall power*
> *A prowd rebellious Unicorn defies.*

Long before the *Faerie Queen* these two animals represented two ancient enemies and were featured on their coats of arms – England and Scotland. Three lions were emblazoned on the royal coat of arms of Richard I. He was known as 'Lionheart' because of his military reputation as a great crusader. The lions symbolised the three areas of the Angevin Kingdom - England, Normandy, and Aquitaine. According to *The Oxford Guide to Heraldry* (1988) by Thomas Woodcock and John Martin Robinson, the oldest documented example of arms on a shield in Europe was recorded by the late 12th century chronicler Jean de Marmentier. In 1127 when Henry I knighted his son-in-law Geoffrey of Anjou, the founder of the Plantagenet dynasty, he hung about his neck a large shield painted with three golden lions. This was possibly an early use of what became the English Royal Coat of Arms and has continued as it's still retained on the shirts of the England football team.

The unicorn, a powerful beast that cannot be tamed, was first used on the Scottish royal coat of arms by William I of Scotland in the 12th century. Jessica Brain, a freelance writer living in Kent, wrote on the website *Historic UK* that the unicorn represented innocence and purity and was associated with chivalry, pride, and boldness. In the 15th century Scottish coins depicted the unicorn. The Mercat Crosses built in several of that nation's towns and cities to symbolise their trading rights incorporated the unicorn. A national Unicorn Day is celebrated on April 9th promoting the national animal of Scotland.

The rivalry between the English Lion and the Scottish Unicorn did not cease when James VI of Scotland united the two crowns and became James I of England in 1603. "Popular tradition," wrote the Opies, "is that the rhyme tells the story of the amalgamation of the Royal Arms of Scotland with those of England ……Two unicorns were supporters of the Scottish royal arms and, with a lion on the other side, one of them became a supporter of the English shield." The Opies pointed out that the new coat of arms showed the lion wearing a crown and the unicorn who was 'merely armed'. This could have given rise to the feeling that they were fighting each other.

In 1707 with the Act of Union in the reign of Queen Anne the two countries were united with a single coat of arms, the lion on one side and the unicorn on the other. Before that the Scottish coat of arms had flaunted two unicorns. Coincidentally or by design, the rhyme was included one year after the union in the satire *Useful Transactions in Philosophy* written by the poet William King in 1708-09. It was in an essay advising learned men how to write "unintelligibly". Although the rhyme may have been circulating some time before then, this is the earliest surviving printed version of it.

Lewis Carroll thought the song was ancient. In Chapter VIII of *Through the Looking Glass* (1871) Alice, repeats to herself "the words of the old song".

But how old? The Opies said they had a copy of a 1638 edition of *The Holy Bible* which had an inscription dated 1691 beside a woodcut of the Royal Arms with the lion and unicorn as 'supporters' placed on either side of a shield. The inscription read: "The unicorn & the lyon fiteing for the Crown and the lyon beat the unicorn Round about the town." I could not however find these lines written beside the woodcut inscription in the 1638 edition of the Opie's Bible in their collection in the Bodleian Library in Oxford!

The rhyme could be a reference to an actual battle between the two nations before the Act of Union. Two other verses give us further clues. The better-known one, mentioned at the start of this chapter, surfaced in an 1805 edition of Benjamin

Tabart's *Songs for the Nursery* and has the lines of the second verse just as they are printed at the top of this chapter. It includes an important clue: 'Some gave them plum-cake'.

The Oxford Companion to Sugar and Sweets, published by the Oxford University Press in 2015, described plum cake as an early type of English fruitcake which emerged in England before 1700. "It took its name from its trove of raisins and currants which the English came to call 'plums' around 1660." We now have an approximate time for the rhyme between say 1650 and 1708 when William King was writing *Transactions of Philosophy*.

The less widely known third verse, which the Opies thought might be older than the verse about the plum cake, appeared in a 'chapbook' (a paper-covered booklet sold by pedlars known as chapmen) called *Vocal Harmony* which was published around 1806. As you can read in the rhyme at the head of this chapter the lion beat the unicorn 'three times over'.

Was there a time when the English beat the Scots 'in and out' in three separate successive battles? Albert Jack thought the rhyme referred to 1745 when Bonnie Prince Charlie landed in Scotland and led a Scottish army south in an attempt to regain the throne from George II. He was at first successful with two victories at Prestonpans and Carlisle. But when he reached Derby his Highland soldiers began to desert him and he had to retreat. He was then decisively beaten at the Battle of Culloden when his forces were butchered by the Duke of Cumberland. Albert Jack's theory must be doubtful because the wrong animal won the first two battles - the Scottish unicorn rather than the English lion! There weren't three successive victories. Also, the date 1745 is suspect because we know the rhyme was current in 1708 – 37 years before the disastrous massacre.

Katherine Elwes Thomas had a more likely timing one century earlier after the victory of the Roundheads' New Model Army at the battle of Naseby on June 14th 1645. The American sleuth wrote: "Charles I as 'the lion', having appealed to Ireland for help, the 'indignant Scotch' as the 'unicorn'.... rallied in immense numbers to the standard of Colonel Oliver Cromwell. This division of forces resulting for a time in 'the lion and the unicorn fighting for the crown'. 'The lion' during the winter, literally beat the unicorn all around the town and during this exciting period they [presumably the defeated soldiers] were given by their respective sympathizers 'white bread and brown' with the finale of plum cake and sent out of town."

I found it hard to equate her description of these events with historical fact. Instead of Charles I (the lion) winning any victories in the winter of 1645, Cromwell's New Model Army swept all before him. The historian Dominic Selwood wrote in the *Daily Telegraph* (14/6/2017) on the anniversary of the Battle of Naseby: "In the aftermath of Naseby, Parliament retook Leicester, then the remaining Royalist strongholds across the south and west. Within a year, King Charles had surrendered."

If the rhyme isn't about Charles I, could it be about his son later Charles II? This was suggested by the American medical doctor and nursery rhyme detective, Albert Mason Stevens, in his book about the origins of eight nursery rhymes published by his widow in 1968. Stevens's research led him to conclude that the first verse was composed in late October 1651. It was about the Battle of Worcester which took place on September 3rd. Oliver Cromwell's New Model Army of 28,000 men defeated the future Charles II's 16,000 Royalists of whom the vast majority were Scottish. The 'lion' was Cromwell, leading the English, and the 'unicorn' was Prince Charles leading the Scots.

According to *Cromwell's Crowning Mercy* by Malcom Atkin (1998) "Cromwell's men were clearly in no mood to show mercy and the fighting in the narrow lanes [of Worcester] was extremely bitter." Richard Baxter, a Puritan preacher who lived nearby in Kidderminster described how the Parliamentary forces entered the city in the failing light of the day and the Scots were "trodden down and slain in the streets". Initial reports showed that between 2000-4000 Scots were killed whereas English losses were estimated to be about 200.

'Some gave them white bread': thousands of Scots were taken prisoner. Stevens found a pamphlet of the time called *Another Victory* quoted by the 19th century historian Samuel Rawson Gardiner in his *History of the Commonwealth and Protectorate* (1894). This described the entry of the prisoners into London. As the "haggard and dispirited" Scots marched past from their long journey the London crowds took pity on them. Friendly hands pressed on them offerings of food and money and some even gave them "good white bread".

'Some gave them plum cake and drummed them out of town': Stevens suggested this might have been a jokey pun and really referred to another 'plumb' meaning lead or bullets. Some of the officers were court-martialled and shot. And 'drumming out of town' was one of the rituals of defeat. It was a brutal description.

'He beat him three times over': the battle of Worcester was one of three unsuccessful attempts by Prince Charles's supporters to capture the Crown. The first was exactly a year earlier (September 3rd 1650) when Cromwell decisively defeated a Scottish army backed by Charles at Dunbar. The second was at Worcester, the same day one year later. And the third victory happened in a major European battle in June 1658 when Cromwell and the French defeated the Spanish and the Scottish at the Battle of the Dunes near Dunkirk. This could have inspired the later line about the third defeat.

Oliver Cromwell, the 'lion' of the rhyme died three months later in 1658 coincidentally also on that date - September 3rd. It took another 240 years before his statue was built in 1899 outside the Houses of Parliament. Next time you pass it take a good look at its pedestal: at its base is a rather black 'lion couchant' with, when I passed it recently, a scattering of dark green mould on its back!

CHAPTER FIVE

LITTLE JACK HORNER

Merry prankster, prig or thief?

> Little Jack Horner sat in a corner,
> Eating a Christmas pie;
> He put in his thumb and pulled out a plum,
> And said: 'What a good boy am I!

Was Little Jack Horner a medieval figure of fun, an opportunist thief in the reign of Henry VIII or a Puritan goody-goody? The most popular theory is that he was a dishonest steward who stole a title deed of a manor concealed in a Christmas pie.

The Horner family descendants who still live in Mells Manor deny the allegation. I went to visit its current head, Raymond Asquith, Lord Oxford, and interviewed him in his kitchen in the picturesque village of Mells on the edge of the Somerset Mendips.

A family's honour is at stake and to get to the bottom of this mystery I started with the earliest surviving reference we have to a pie-eating Jack Horner. It goes back to 1725 when Henry Carey (an anti-Whig poet) wrote *Namby Pamby*. This was a work (mentioned in my introduction) satirising Ambrose Philips, a staunch Whig and writer of pastoral poems, who was fond of sending nursery jingles to the children of his sponsors:

> *Now he sings of Jacky Horner,*
> *Sitting in the chimney corner,*
> *Eating of a Christmas pie,*
> *Putting in his thumb, O fie!*
> *Putting in, O fie! his thumb,*
> *Pulling out, O strange, a plum.*

Few people realise that this incident about eating a pie and pulling out a plum appears in a much longer ballad about a 'merrie prankster'. The four lines (quoted at the top of this chapter) were included in a chapbook. *The Pleasant History of Jack Horner* described the "witty tricks and pleasant pranks" that Jack played from his youth to his "riper years" in which he was given a coat which made him invisible and magic pipes which he played so well that crowds danced in the streets.

The oldest surviving copy of this 'pleasant' history dates from 1764. It came to eight chapters over 24 pages in a twopenny 1790 edition which I found in the British Library. Its most famous lines are clearly shown on the first and title page of the booklet. In the narrative itself the incident appears in the middle of the first chapter which describes his birth and education.

The Opies thought that the inclusion of the plum pie lines in the chapbook version of the *History of Jack Horner* was exceedingly awkward. They wrote: "It seems clear that they have been dragged in, probably as a peg on which to hang the tale. This is in the tradition of chapbook literature."

Reading the first chapter it's possible to see how they came to this conclusion. The narrative describes Jack as a "pretty boy of curious wit. All people spoke his praise". Then the Christmas pie incident is described: "And in the corner would he sit, in Christmas holidays……." One can see how a pamphleteer faced with a long and incongruous ballad could have spiced it up by advertising its most famous lines on the title page and then interspersing them into the narrative.

The main burden of the ballad which is extremely bawdy in parts does not fit in easily with the "good boy" in the rhyme. Chapter III has little Jack fighting a servant maid who raps him on the crown with a "baisting ladle" and then "piss'd upon his head and put out both his eyes" while he bites her "by the arse". All very unpleasant. But Chapter VII has even worse. Jack dancing naked ("save smock and shirt") in the street, having spent the night with an innkeeper's wife and a quaker when all three became stuck in a chamber pot!

One clue to his identity is his height. Little Jack was indeed very little:

When he to age was come,
As being thirteen inches high,
A giant to Tom Thumb

And in the lusty fight with the serving maid the author mentions again that Jack was but thirteen inches high and she was "five times more".

James Orchard Halliwell, the great collector of nursery rhymes, claimed an ancient pedigree for the rhyme. In his 1842 collection he included the short verse about the pie and linked it to an ancient tale. Citing the lines at the top of this chapter he wrote: "The tale of Jack Horner has long been appropriated to the nursery. The four lines which follow are the traditional ones, and they form part of 'The pleasant History of Jack Horner, containing his witty Tricks and pleasant Pranks, which he plaied from his Youth to his riper Years', a copy of which is in the Bodleian Library." Halliwell later wrote that this extended story is in substance the same as "The Fryer and the Boy, London 1617, and both of them are taken from the more ancient story of 'Jack and his Step-dame', which has been printed by Mr Wright."

Mother Goose's Melody was written and printed by John Newbery at about the same time as the ballad was seen in London around 1760. It contained only the Christmas pie lines of the nursery rhyme. A joke beneath the poem suggested that Jack might have been "apprenticed to a mince pye-maker",

Percy B. Green, who wrote *A History of Nursery Rhymes* (1899) included the Jack Horner rhyme in his category of 'Jack Rhymes'. He recalled the great legendary Jacks including Jack and the Beanstalk and Jack the Giant Killer which were translated into Latin by Geoffrey of Monmouth and found in Scandinavian folklore.

He wrote that Little Jack Horner had nothing to do with the prankster. The rhyme about him was another of the Jack-rhyming nursery classics which sprang into being after the Civil War (1642-1651) when Parliament was in the ascendancy, theatres and public gardens were closed, and maypoles, wakes, fairs, church music, dancing and puppet shows banned. Looking back at an erstwhile golden age for children, he observed: "The pastimes of all classes, but more especially those of the lower orders who had been so happy under the Tudor sovereigns, suffered a miserable suspension."

He went on: "The rhyme recording Jack Horner's gloomy conduct was, in fact, a satire on Puritanical aversion to Christmas activities." The lines about the Christmas pie in his version are at the front of the rhyme which begins:

Jack Horner was a pretty lad, near London he did dwell,
His father's heart he made full glad, his mother loved him well,
A pretty boy of curious wit, all people spoke his praise,
And in a corner he would sit on Christmas Holy-days.
When friends they did together meet to pass away the time,
Why, little Jack, he sure would eat his Christmas pie in rhyme,
And say: 'Jack Horner, in the corner, eats good Christmas pie,
And with his thumb pulls out a plum,
Saying what a good boy am I.

I could find little about Percy B Green. He's not mentioned among the notable figures connected with nursery rhymes in the index of the celebrated Opies's dictionary. Yet Green's history covers a whole gamut of them. Jack rhymes is but one category. Others are games, riddles, cat rhymes, cradle songs, money rhymes, scraps, songs and scotch rhymes. His last section is devoted to nursery rhymes with 'a political significance'. Most of these date to the 17th century and the rows between Royalists and Puritans. The first one referred to the coronation of Charles II and begins:

Come, Jack, let's drink a pot of ale,
And I shall tell thee such a tale
Will make thine ears to ring.

It was, he said, "a Roundhead sneer at the man after the Royalist rejoicings were over". Political debate hedged in jingles which later became nursery rhymes were common and *Little Jack Horner* was one of them. However, it wasn't long before he soon ceased to be a figure of fun or a Puritan goody goody and gained a reputation as an opportunist rogue.

In 1731 just six years after Carey wrote *Namby Pamby* Little Jack Horner featured in Henry Fielding's play *The Grub Street Opera.* This was an attack on the prime minister Robert Walpole and ended with all the characters trooping off the stage "to the music of Little Jack Horner" and singing: "What happy rogues are we!"

In 1796 the Reverend Samuel Bishop, poet and headmaster of Merchant Taylors' School, London, ridiculed Civil Service bureaucracy in his *Epigram XXII* as follows:

> *What are they but JACK HORNERS, who snug in their corners,*
> *Cut freely the public pie?*
> *Till each with his thumb has squeezed out a round Plum,*
> *Then he cries, "What a Great Man am I!*

In 1817 the writer Thomas Love Peacock referred to the Christmas pie in his satirical novel *Melincourt* about five swindling traders:

> *Jack Horner's CHRISTMAS PIE my learned nurse*
> *Interpreted to mean the public purse.*
> *From thence a plum he drew. O happy Horner!*
> *Who would not be ensconced in thy snug corner?*

Each in turn then described the nature of his sharp practice in his particular profession, followed by the general chorus:

> *And we'll all have a finger, a finger, a finger,*
> *We'll all have a finger in the CHRISTMAS PIE."*

How did a merry bawdy prankster or possibly a young Puritan prig get this reputation for opportunism? At the time of the dissolution of the monasteries a Thomas Horner was a steward to the last abbot of Glastonbury, Richard Whiting. It is alleged that the abbot sent Master Horner to King Henry VIII in 1539 with the deeds of Mells Manor and 11 other properties concealed in a Christmas pie as a goodwill gesture to prevent the king from dissolving the abbey. Horner travelled up to town in the abbot's wagon. At some point during his journey he lifted the crust of the pie, picked one document out and stole it – the deeds of the Manor of Mells. When Horner returned he told the abbot that the king had given the manor to him.

The story about the deeds being concealed in a pie is not as fanciful as it might seem. In chapter 12 (*Sing a Song of Sixpence*) I will explain how Tudor pies were constructed on the outside with thick layers of crust. They were hollow in the middle and the tops were left open so that chefs could place birds, frogs, dogs, dwarves and even on one occasion a small band of players in them. The hiding of manorial deeds inside a pie would have been a small matter in comparison. However, if it was to be taken on a 130-mile or more journey in a wagon the pie couldn't have been that large or else it would have aroused suspicions!

Thomas Horner's master, Richard Whiting, then aged nearly 80, was later arrested by Henry VIII and tried for robbing Glastonbury Abbey of 200,000 crowns and concealing other treasures. One book by Thomas Becket was found in his possession which was illegal as he had sided with the pope against his king. Another book found in the Abbey defended Catherine of Aragon and argued against the grounds for Henry's divorce. A local jury was hastily formed and it included Thomas Horner.

Edward Watson described in *The Last Abbot of Glastonbury & other essays* (1908) how: "Friends and allies turned against the Abbot for a share in the rich booty to be had at the Abbey." No defence was allowed, and the abbot was found guilty on November 14th 1539. The next day, despite his old age, the abbot was cruelly hung, drawn and quartered on Glastonbury Tor.

The Opies wrote that from a historical angle there was "no objection to the short rhyme having referred to the Horner ancestor". Anyone who was believed to be a knave might have been called Jack. They said: "Glastonbury at the beginning of 1539 was the only religious house in Somerset left untouched and it was the richest abbey in the kingdom. When Abbot Whiting was on trial for his life, Thomas Horner was a member of the complaisant jury which condemned him. It is admitted that Horner benefited by being a King's man, and the local people may well have had their own ideas about how he acquired his estates." Later they added: "It is on record also that in the relevant period Whiting several times sent Christmas gifts to the King…" The Opies went on to point out: "It may be stressed, however, that the legend which has now become so firmly attached to the rhyme has not been found in print before the nineteenth century."

The earliest version we have of the 'manorial plum pie' incident appeared more than 300 years after the dissolution of the monasteries (1536-41) . It is dated 30/1/1858 in *Notes & Queries*. This was a weekly journal started nine years earlier in London to encourage academics and others to exchange notes and queries about folklore, literature, and other matters. A correspondent with the initials A.D.C. reported what he or she had heard about the nursery rhyme from an old lady in Somerset.

The old lady had said that Jack Horner, who was from a poor family, was chosen to carry the title deeds of Glastonbury Abbey - which were hidden in a pie - to the King's Commissioners. On the way he felt hungry and dipped into the pie's crust and although he could not read or understand the documents, he extracted one. When he delivered his parcel it was "perceived that one of the chief deeds (the deeds of the Mells Abbey estates) was missing". The abbot was sent for and executed on the grounds that he had withheld it. But after "the monasteries were despoiled" the parchment with the deeds was found in the possession of Jack Horner and "that was the plum which little Jack Horner unwittingly had become possessed of ".

According to Raymond Asquith, Lord Oxford, who is descended 14 generations down from Thomas Horner's brother John, it took a few years for the story in *Notes & Queries* to be connected directly to his family. He remembers his grandmother, Katharine Asquith (née Horner) telling him that the first time the family had been linked to the rhyme was about 140 years ago in the 1880s. His great-grandmother Frances Graham Horner, a well-known Liberal, married John Horner, the owner of Mells Manor in 1883. She had a reputation as an *avant-garde* hostess. The *Oxford Dictionary of National Biography* recorded that she was one of the first young unmarried women in London to entertain her own guests!

Dr K.D. Reynolds, the historian and expert on Victorian aristocracy, wrote the *ODNB* article. She said Edward Burne-Jones the celebrated pre-Raphaelite artist, who painted a number of portraits of Frances, "developed a passion" for her and was in despair when she married someone he termed a 'market-gardener'.

John Fortescue Horner was a lawyer and a keen cricketer who played for the MCC (Marylebone Cricket Club). He was later knighted when he served as Commissioner of the Crown's Forest and Woodlands, which is a far cry from market gardens! Lord Oxford was also told by his grandmother that John (Fortescue) was also known as 'Jack' and "some catty armchair historians thought his wife was making social and political waves beyond her status and wanted to bring her down a little".

Katherine Elwes Thomas found a mention of the story in a footnote in *The Orrery Papers* edited by Emily Charlotte, Countess of Cork and Orrery, and published in

1903. This was in reference to a letter from John Boyle, 5th Earl of Cork and Orrery, dated 18th January 1739 to a Mrs Strangways Horner (who married a descendant of the family and lived in Mells Manor).

It made no reference to the rhyme but the footnote from the editor said that Mrs Horner resided at Mells Park. It had a slightly different slant on the tale with the deeds being offered by Henry VIII to the abbot and not *vice versa*: "The majority of readers are probably unacquainted with the fact that the familiar nursery stanza *Little Jack Horner* was originally a political squib. The 'Jack Horner' of the day, being sent by the King with a grant of land to the Abbots of Glastonbury, on the way thither abstracted the 'plum' in question, viz: the deed gift of Mells Park. The slowness of inquiries of distant communications in those times, delayed discovery of the fraud, so that 'possession proved nine points of the law' to some purpose for the felonious Jack."

Like Agatha Christie's Miss Marple, who was solving a murder at St Mary Mead, her fictional vicarage at the time, Ms Thomas, the author of *The Real Personages of Mother Goose* (1930), made a special train journey to Mells Station in Somerset and walked across hawthorn-edged fields through the village to what she called 'Horner Hall'. She was invited to stay for dinner by three Misses Horner. Afterwards they took her to the library and showed her books which contained the political skit on Sir John Horner but they insisted that Little Jack Horner not only presented the Christmas pie intact to the monarch but later bought the property. The family had the original manorial deed bearing Henry VIII's signature.

I went to the Tudor manor in February 2023. Here proudly displayed in the reception hall, were the original deeds of the conveyance. They are in a golden frame with the royal signature and dangling seal tied at the bottom. At the top a large capital H encircles a drawing of a splendidly robed King Henry sitting on his throne and carrying a sceptre and orb. The title deeds are still in pristine condition, no pie stains, just faint horizontal folds across the parchment. I measured them: 30 inches by 19 inches – surely too large for any humble steward to smuggle in a pie all the way from Glastonbury to London, and in no way crumpled or showing any signs of having been squashed into it!

The deeds were dated 10th July 1543. They covered thousands of acres and included lands in Leigh-on-Mendip, Cloford and Doulting, now the Shepton Mallet showground for the annual Bath and West Show, some six miles away from Mells.

The price declared in the deeds was £1831,19 shillings, 11 pence and one 'obol'. This was a medieval description of a halfpenny according to Albert Peel, the 20th century Congregationist and historian. Lord Oxford commented: "It has been pretty minutely valued and Henry never knowingly undersold!" According to the Bank of England's inflation calculator this figure amounts to at least £1½ million today.

The sale was listed among the grants made in July 1543 in the *Foreign and Domestic Papers* of Henry VIII published by His Majesty's Stationery Office (1901). The recipients were described as Thomas and John Horner Junior. The price was stated as £1831 19s 11¾p – a farthing more! It included the manors of "Melles, Lyne and Nonney" as well as some "advowsons" and a pension of 20s out of the Melles rectory. It was also dated July 10th.

The transfer of land was confirmed by John Leyland, the Tudor antiquarian, who Lord Oxford suspects may have been an agent of the king reporting back to him on the sale of former monastic lands. Leyland visited Mells that year (1543) and reported: "There is a praty maner place of stone harde at the west ende of the churche. This be likelihood was partely builded by Abbate Selwodde of Glastinbryi. Sins it served the farmer of thye lordship. Now Mr Horner hath boute the lordship of the King."

How did a poor steward get the wherewithal to buy such a vast collection of properties and land? Sitting with a cup of tea in the manor kitchen I was taken back to those heady 16th century days when nearby Frome was the largest town in Somerset. Lord Oxford said: "The Mendip area was steeped in wool, and had a huge flourishing trade which included London, Antwerp, Ghent and Bruges. Many people in the area were called 'Clothier'. There were 100 wool mills in Mells which derived its name from the medieval Latin name for mills 'milnes'."

The Horners were, he went on, well established in the area some time before the dissolution of the monasteries. The dissolution sparked a massive land grab and nowhere more so than in southeast Somerset when the vast properties owned by the Abbey of Glastonbury went up for sale. In his large library which houses the family archives Lord Oxford has ledgers listing letters patent and other evidence to show that Thomas Horner went on to buy Cloford Manor from a Mr Basyng in about 1544 and about that time Charterhouse Manor on top of the Mendips. Parcels of land all around the Mells area were sold to the Horners. "It was the biggest transfer of land in our island's history," Lord Oxford said. It was referred to in a county jingle which the Opies dated back to the 17th century and was included by G.F. Northall in his 1892 collection of *English Folk Rhymes*:

> *Horner, Popham, Wyndham and Thynne,*
> *When the monks went out, then they went in.*

An early record in his library refers to a Robert Horner Esquire, possibly Thomas's father, signing a 'quitclaim' or a release of their right to a 'toft' or tenement in Leigh-on-Mendip in 1482.

Alice Blows, an architectural historian and authority on Mells Manor, wrote about the family in *Mells Manor and the Houses of the Horners* (2020): "The Horners were evidently connected both with Mells and Glastonbury Abbey in the late fifteenth and early sixteenth century which may explain why they moved quickly to secure the house following the dissolution."

As far back as 1912 the county historians G W & J H Wade, authors of *Rambles in Somerset*, discounted a popular tale that Little Jack was a scullion in the Glastonbury Abbey kitchens. "Unfortunately for the truth of the story, the Horner who first acquired the estates was not a lad but a gentleman of means and his name was Jack not Thomas. As the King needed money he was anxious to obtain purchasers for the monastic lands, and Thomas Horner, who had previously rented the estate under the Abbey, and whose loyalty had been favourably mentioned by the Commissioners, came forward as the buyer for Mells….."

Robert Dunning, the Somerset historian, in his book *Somerset Families* (2002) wrote: "Historians usually marvel how John Horner, although bailiff of Glastonbury Abbey's manor of Mells, could possibly have found the huge sum of £1831 19s ½d to pay to the Crown for the former abbey manors of Mells, Leigh-on-Mendip and Nunney. A 'plum' certainly but hints have been dropped that the transaction may not have been entirely above suspicion and that the piecrust hid a doubtfully-acquired deed of title.

"But two John Horners, one called the elder and one of Stoke Michael, were at least in the 1530s, the years covered by the account books of the international cloth dealer Sir Thomas Kytson, deeply involved in the cloth business. The first was called cloth broker and cloth worker and dealt not only in white (undyed) English cloth but also in Bruges satin and sarcenet [a fine soft fabric] and imported woad. John of Stoke produced kersies [coarse cloth] for the Flemish market and also bought in woad. There was money in cloth worth investing in land."

Lord Oxford, who readily admits that his ancestor participated in and after a few years benefitted from the execution of the old abbot, regrets that his family has been plagued for years with the theft story. He and his father were interviewed about it on the radio. He says wistfully: "It's pretty uphill work trying to get this kind of myth out of the bloodstream of the country."

Although there is impeccable evidence that his family did not steal the property, the rumour could still have been spread by a lampoon at the time that has become one of our best-known nursery rhymes. But why did it take nearly 330 years (from the 1539 dissolution of the abbey to the 1868 collection of folklore anecdotes) to emerge in print? The young pretty boy described as sitting down at the table in a corner is a somewhat far cry from an adolescent steward travelling in a horse-drawn wagon. And why did they not use his proper name 'Thomas' rather than Jack? As Lord Oxford pointed out to me: "The rhyme could have equally gone 'Little Tom Horner' with no loss to the scansion."

The medieval ballad theory is a bit odd. The inclusion of the pie incident appears incongruous with the rest of the ballad. Not only that: how could a person who was only 13 inches high put a plum in his mouth and pull it out with such decorum?

The best explanation so far is the one by Percy B Green that this is one of the famous Jack rhymes. Jack be nimble, Jack and Jill and Jack Sprat. Little Jack Horner's name was used to lampoon a smug young prig by pro-Royalists after the Civil War to pour fun on the Puritans' dislike of Christmas celebrations. It was a Cavalier's song of derision at the straight-laced Puritan which was probably interspersed into a bawdy ballad to increase its sale and then much later used as ammunition to denigrate a reputable manor owner whose wife seemed to some to be 'better than she ought to be'.

CHAPTER SIX

LITTLE MISS MUFFET

Thomas the Spiderman

Little Miss Muffet
Sat on a tuffet,
Eating her curds and whey;
There came a big spider,
Who sat down beside her
And frightened Miss Muffet away.

The Scottish version for the origin of this rhyme has little Miss Muffet as Mary Queen of Scots. If it had been the title of a play this was how the central character would have been cast by Katherine Elwes Thomas in her book *The Real Personages of Mother Goose* published in 1930.

She was sure that the young Mary Stuart, aged 18, was the little arachnophobe, and set the scene. It was June 1560. Mary's first husband, Francis II King of France, had died. She had returned to Scotland and was sitting on a tuffet (three-legged stool) in the grounds of Holyrood Palace in Edinburgh. As she was eating her curds and whey (a Tudor milky dish we now call junket), a big spider called John Knox sat down beside her.

The Rev John Knox, founder of the Presbyterian Church of Scotland, was the leader of the Scottish Reformation. He was the fiery author of the pamphlet: *The First Blast of the Trumpet against The Monstrous Regiment of Women* (1558). Mary was said by Linda Alchin to have been so scared of him that she confided: "I'll fear the prayers of John Knox more than all the assembled armies of Europe."

But I couldn't find this quotation in any of the biographies I consulted of Mary Stuart or of John Knox. Antonia Fraser in *Mary Queen of Scots* (1969) recorded that before she set foot in Scotland the new queen told the English ambassador, Sir Nicholas Throckmorton, she believed Knox to "be the most dangerous man in the kingdom". But far from being frightened of him she was "determined to grasp the nettle". She sent for Knox to come to Holyrood. There were at least five recorded meetings between the two. Although they sometimes drove Mary to tears, they also caused her to laugh at him and were always at Mary's prompting or instigation.

Little Miss Muffet first appeared in *Songs for the Nursery* which was printed in 1805 for Benjamin Tabart, the English publisher and bookseller, who operated from Bond Street, London. The words in the rhyme have hardly changed through the ages but there is one perhaps crucial difference in the 1808 edition of the *Songs* which I was able to look at in the Bodleian Library and which I have underlined. It might make the giant of the Scottish reformation an unlikely spider suspect:

Little Miss Muffet,
She sat on a tuffet,
Eating of curds and whey,
There came a <u>little</u> spider,
Who sat down beside her,
And frightened Miss Muffet away.

Although John Knox was described by an Edinburgh citizen, Sir Peter Young, writing in 1579, 15 years after Knox's death, as "rather below the normal height", his countenance, "which was grave and stern, though not harsh, bore a natural dignity and air of authority: in anger his frown became imperious". This description is a far cry from 'a little spider'.

Why was the unfortunate Miss ever called Muffet? Was it just to rhyme with tuffet? What exactly was the real meaning of 'tuffet' when the rhyme surfaced in 1805? It comes down to whether it means a 'footstool' as translated by Katherine Thomas or a 'grassy mound or hillock'.

Was there a real family called Muffet who had anything to do with spiders? Because if there was, it might be a much better explanation for the origin of the rhyme than the Scottish one. Most modern nursery rhyme interpreters, including Linda Alchin,

Albert Jack, Sandy Leong and Diana Ferguson, point to Thomas Muffet, Moffet or Moufet, who was born in Shoreditch, London, in 1553.

Son of a haberdasher, a seller of buttons etc, he attended Merchant Taylors' School in London before going on to Cambridge University. He qualified as a Doctor of Medicine at Basel University in Switzerland at the age of 25. He then spent a year studying silkworms in Italy.

Professor Victor Houliston, the literary historian and biographer, described how Moffet was very vigorous in spreading the practice of a modern and very controversial form of alternative medicine known as 'paracelsianism' in England. This was named after a 16th century physician and alchemist called Paracelsus who introduced the idea of applying chemicals, minerals and even poisons to medicine.

In an article in the journal *Medical History* (1989) called *Sleepers Awake: Thomas Moffet's Challenge to the College of Physicians,* Houliston related how Moffet, a staunch Puritan, became personal physician to Mary Herbert, Countess of Pembroke, sister of the famous poet and courtier Sir Philip Sidney. Through the Herberts and Sidneys he attracted the attention of some of the most famous courtiers of that time. The Earl of Essex, Sir Francis Walsingham and Sir Francis Drake were among his patients.

After a long struggle because of his unusual medical opinions, Dr Muffet became a Fellow of the Royal College of Physicians in 1580. One of his great London friends was Thomas Penny, a fellow doctor and entomologist, who suffered from asthma and treated it with doses of woodlice crushed in wine. Together they collated their writings and those of other distinguished entomologists. The result was a definitive Latin work: *Theatrum Insectorum*. This was an illustrated guide to the classification and lives of insects illustrated with hundreds of woodcut paintings. Four chapters of this extensive work were devoted to spiders.

Philip H Swann, an expert on spiders, wrote in the *Bulletin of the British Arachnological Society* (1973): "The section on spiders in the *Theatrum* probably shows the influence of Mouffet on his sources more strongly than any other part of the book … we still have a very vivid insight into the way a sixteenth century man of Science saw spiders. The natural world for Mouffet was finite and created by God as a static entity. His interest in animals is largely confined to his desire to demonstrate their didactic and utilitarian purpose."

It seems crazy now and must have seemed at least eccentric then: Dr Muffet recommended spiders to cure toothache following instructions first put forward by Pliny the Elder in his *Natural History* (AD 77). You had to catch a spider with your left hand, bruise it in oil of roses and drop the juice into the ear on the same side as the toothache. A spider and its thread laid on the navel could relieve constipation but if the spider had been captured while it is climbing up its thread, it could treat diarrhea!

Muffet was also besotted with the beauty of spiders: "The skin of it is so soft, smooth, polished and neat, that she precedes the softest skin'd Mayds [maids], and the daintiest and most beautiful strumpets …."

He thought they were special gifts of God: "Who would not admire so great a force, so great weight, so sharp and hard bitings, and almost incredible strength in so small a body, and of no consideration, having neither bones, nerves, flesh and hardly any skin? This cannot proceed from its body, but its spirit; or rather God himself." Muffet was so obsessed with spiders that he could easily have been made fun of particularly when the popularity of Paracelsianism declined in the 17th century.

The main objection to the rhyme being inspired by 'Spiderman Thomas' was based on the work of Lina Eckenstein, author of *Comparative Studies in Nursery Rhymes* (1906). She included *Little Miss Muffet* in the category of cushion dances like *Joan Saunderson* and *Sally Sanders*. John Playford's *The Dancing Master* (1651) described how a male dancer came into a room carrying a cushion. He danced around the room looking for a girl to dance with. When he found one, he placed the cushion in front of her and they both knelt on the cushion.

Similar poems to *Little Miss Muffet* sound as if they were cushion dances. For example Lina Eckenstein cited two which she said appeared in 1842 nearly 30 years after Muffet. They were *Little Miss Mopsey* and *Little Mary Ester*. The latter went as follows:

> *Little Mary Ester, sat upon a tester [footstool],*
> *Eating of curds and whey;*
> *There came a little spider*
> *And sat down beside her*
> *And frightened Mary Ester away.*

"Tuffet and tester are words for a footstool," wrote Eckenstein. However in 1805 (the earliest date we have for the nursery rhyme) it is unlikely that the word 'tuffet' meant 'a three-legged stool' on which a cushion might have been put. *Brewer's Dictionary of Phrase and Fable* classified 'tuffet' as a dialect variant of 'tuft' meaning a small 'grassy mound or hillock' and quoted the nursery rhyme in this connection. There was no mention of tuffet ever being a footstool.

The *Oxford English Dictionary* dates the tuft meaning back to 1553 and the hillock or mound meaning back to 1877. It dates the hassock or footstool meaning to 1895 but the OED explained that this was a doubtful meaning "due to a misunderstanding of the nursery rime [sic] which may belong to sense 2. [hillock]."

If the *OED* is right, then it's likely that 'tuffet' was chosen to rhyme with 'muffet'. And why 'muffet'? It could only have been chosen because the rhyme was about a relation of the spider expert.

In 1999 Bernard Taylor, an engineer, bought a five-bedroom twin-gabled house, conspicuous by its antiquity in the mock Tudor stockbroker belt of commuter suburbia in North Mymms about 17 miles north of the City of London. Thirty-nine years earlier it had been saved from demolition by the parish council. There was nothing in the title deeds to show how old his new still dilapidated home was but when he lifted some of the wide oaken floor planks in one of the bedrooms he found old acorns and leaves which had been put there for insulation. Down in the cellars he found a well, perhaps 20 to 30 meters deep, and its clear water revealed unmistakable Tudor brickwork.

A central square portion of the large rambling house in a long winding road called Moffat's Lane in Brookmans Park is genuine Tudor. Its oak beams are dented with cracks for wattle and daub, and interspersed with holes so that wooden poles could be used to truss them up firmly. A large brick wide oak-beamed fireplace has brick oven recesses. When they were being shown around the house for the first time his wife Elizabeth spotted a large iron-cast spider by the fireplace. But when they took possession, it was nowhere to be seen. A few weeks later they noticed a group of primary school children peering through the windows headed by their teacher describing the house. The children, from the local Brookmans Park Primary School, were wearing uniforms with badges incorporating a spider's web.

Word in the local area is that Thomas Muffet lived at Moffat's Farm and his daughter Patience came down into the kitchen one morning and was scared when she saw a little spider. So he composed the poem as a joke.

With the help of local historians working for the North Mymms Local History Project, Bernard was able to identify the house, now called Moffat's Farm, as Walter's House, a name it retained until the 19th century. One of the historians, Bill Killick, had unearthed a rental statement from nearby Brookman Manor which mentioned a tenement or holding called 'Waltarres' which was dated April 28th 1536, and was in the Court Rolls of Henry VIII. Bill Killick also explored North Mymms parish church records and discovered the names of Morflett and Murfler among male baptisms in 1565 and 1567.

In 1584 a 'William Murfett' came to the manor's court and acknowledged that "he holds freely of the Lord of this Manor one messuage with curtilage, orchard and gardens called Walters in the parish of Northmymme". Killick also found a deed recording that in 1605 William Moffat, a citizen and skinner of London, sold Walters to his dad, also called William. But when his father died in 1616 a 'William Moffett' sold the house to a William Carter.

If Thomas Muffet lived in the house it would have been between 1588 and 1597. He came back from the Continent to Cambridge in 1582 and according to his entry in the *Dictionary of National Biography* he worked first in Ipswich and later in London where he had a good practice as a physician in 1588. His first wife Jane died in 1600 and was buried in Wilton. So it seems the family moved to Wiltshire when Moffat became MP for Wilton in 1597. He remarried a lady called Catherine Browne who was the mother of two daughters and two sons.

But the marriage did not last that long as the good doctor died on 5th June 1604. He was buried near his first wife in Wilton Church. A few months later, according to the *DNB*, his will was published in November. It clearly showed that he had a brother called William, as he was one of the document's overseers. Thomas's daughter Patience is listed as one of the recipients. His widow Catherine died at Calne, Wiltshire in 1626. Her will on June 26th of that year left a portrait of 'Moffett' and one of his books – probably not the one about spiders - to 'his daughter Patience'.

CHAPTER SEVEN

LONDON BRIDGE

Who was My Fair Lady?

London Bridge is broken down,
Broken down, broken down.
London Bridge is broken down,
My fair lady.

Build it up with wood and clay,
Wood and clay, wood and clay,
Build it up with wood and clay,
My fair lady.

Wood and clay will wash away,
Wash away, wash away,
Wood and clay will wash away,
My fair lady.

Build it up with bricks and mortar,
Bricks and mortar, bricks and mortar,
Build it up with bricks and mortar,
My fair lady.

Bricks and mortar will not stay,
Will not stay, will not stay,
Bricks and mortar will not stay,
My fair lady.

Build it up with iron and steel,
Iron and steel, iron and steel,
Build it up with iron and steel,
My fair lady.

Iron and steel will bend and bow,
Bend and bow, bend and bow,
Iron and steel will bend and bow,
My fair lady.

Build it up with silver and gold,
Silver and gold,
Build it up with silver and gold,
My fair lady.

Silver and gold will be stolen away,
Stolen away, stolen away,
Silver and gold will be stolen away,
My fair lady.

> Set a man to watch all night,
> Watch all night, watch all night,
> Set a man to watch all night,
> My fair lady.
>
> Suppose the man should fall asleep,
> Fall asleep, fall asleep,
> Suppose the man should fall asleep?
> My fair lady.
>
> Give him a pipe to smoke all night,
> Smoke all night, smoke all night,
> Give him a pipe to smoke all night,
> My fair lady.

Don't think of London Bridge as it is now! Conjure up in your mind's eye Old London Bridge (1209-1831), our own *Ponte Vecchio*, much busier and grander than the Florentine version. This was brilliantly brought to life by Patricia Pierce in her book, *Old London Bridge* (2001). Her descriptions of its chapel, its waterworks, its 19 piers and 20 arches, the bustle of its 100 plus shops and at least 140 homes are almost virtual reality in print!

But disaster struck and the bridge fell or broke down. When did this happen? Who was the mysterious 'my fair lady'? And most intriguing of all has this poem anything to do with ritual sacrifices of children and the burial of their bones beneath the foundations?

The Opies believed it had! They were the most cautious of people yet their comment about the poem was, for them, a little short of shocking. They claimed: "It is one of the few, [nursery rhymes] perhaps the only one, in which there is justification for suggesting that it preserves the memory of a dark and terrible rite of past times; and the literary history of the song does not frustrate the idea of its antiquity."

What brought them to this extraordinary conclusion? In France, Germany and Italy, there have been collapsing bridge songs and dances for centuries, and games in which the two sides are often angels and devils going to heaven or hell. These predated the earliest mention in England when a London Bridge dance was mentioned in *The London Chaunticleres*, a witty anonymous comedy printed in the 1650s. In it a dairy woman called Curds said: "I have been one in my daies when we kept the Whitson-Ale where we danc't the building of London-Bridge upon wool-packs." This was a reference to the duty on wool levied to repair the bridge.

In 1894 the folklorist Alice Bertha (Lady) Gomme first connected the old dance to a game of ritual sacrifice. She published many different versions of the song in Volume I of *The Traditional Games of England, Scotland and Ireland*. Four of them contained the extra lines:

> *What has this poor prisoner done*
> *Stole my watch and lost my key*
> *Off to prison he must go.*

Lady Gomme concluded: "Looking to the fact of the widespread superstition of the foundation sacrifice, it would seem that we may have here a tradition of this rite....... and there is a tradition about London Bridge itself, that the stones were bespattered with the blood of little children."

Lewis Spence included a reference to this 'tradition' in his book *Myth and Ritual in Dance, Game and Rhyme* (1947). He wrote: "It is of course well-known that when ancient bridges or buildings of any sort were erected a victim of some kind was usually required by the *genius loci*, or spirit of the locality, as a 'tithe' or blood sacrifice. Moreover, a tradition existed that when London Bridge was built it was 'sanctified' or 'insured' by the blood of children."

Some time earlier, Dr Henry Bett, the author of *Nursery Rhymes and Tales* (1924), was also convinced the rhyme had a murky past. He wrote: "Now, the game *London Bridge is Broken Down*, and the rhyme which accompanies it, preserve unmistakeable traces of human sacrifice at the building of a bridge. There are many variants, but they nearly all agree in these suggestive particulars – the bridge has fallen down and attempts to build it up with different materials are all failures, whereupon there follows – with an apparent lack of connexion – the arrest of a prisoner."

He described how humans were sacrificed as a "propitiation" to the spirits of the earth or water at the foundation of a bridge. He recalled some incidences of this in Polynesia, Bosnia, Serbia, Russia, Greece and Turkey. In the Peloponnese, for example, a bridge kept falling down each night until a bird sang out that it would never be completed until the wife of the master mason was buried in its foundations.

Despite Lady Gomme's claim about stones bespattered with children's blood, no bones of children have so far been found under the foundations of the modern London Bridge or under those of its medieval and Roman predecessors. Patricia Pierce mentioned no human sacrifices in her book. The massive *Chronicles of London Bridge*, written by the antiquary Richard Thomson in 1827, mentioned ancient Roman sacrifices in connection with bridges but never suggested this happened with London Bridge. His chronicles covered every aspect of the bridge's history, over 710 pages.

John Clark, Curator Emeritus of the Museum of London Archaeological Collections Department, wrote in an article on the internet on 18/12/2014: "Like her husband, the historian and folklorist George Laurence Gomme, Mrs Gomme followed the then fashionable practice of finding a very early origin for recent popular beliefs and customs in 'primitive' or 'pagan' ritual – they were too ready, perhaps, to accept, on the basis of 'tradition', that there was a widespread 'fact' of human sacrifices placed in the foundations of bridges and other buildings." Later in the article he pointed to the lack of any evidence to back up Alice Gomme's claims of child sacrifice and adds "I have not identified her source or any independent account of this tradition."

The link between a captured prisoner and a sacrificial rite seems tenuous to me. The closest lines to someone being sacrificed were quoted by Albert Jack in *Pop Goes the Weasel* (2008). He included another verse of the rhyme which might suggest internment:

> *Take a key and lock her up,*
> *Lock her up, lock her up*
> *Take a key and lock her up*
> *My fair lady.*

However this verse is not found in any of Lady Gomme's versions, nor was it quoted by the Opies. Nor was it included in the earliest surviving printed version of *London Bridge* in *Tommy Thumb's Pretty Song Book* published by Mary Cooper in or around 1744. The earliest rhyme had the refrain "Dance over my Lady Lee … with a gay Lady". It did include a watchman and ended:

> *Then we'll set a Man to Watch,*
> *With a gay Lady.*

But there is nothing about giving the watchman a pipe ('to smoke all night' - see last verse of the rhyme at the start of this chapter) which might have dated the poem to sometime after tobacco was first brought to England by Sir Walter Raleigh possibly in 1586. There is no obvious line alluding to sacrifice in the oldest surviving version of the rhyme and the sacrificial theory should be discounted.

The song of *London Bridge* is older than 1744. It was one of the nursery rhymes mentioned by Henry Carey in *Namby Pamby,* in his 1725 skit on nursery rhymes:

> *Namby-Pamby is no clown,*
> *London-Bridge is broken down:*
> *Now he courts the gay ladee,*
> *Dancing o'er the lady-Lee.*

But it is probably much older than that. Writing in the London monthly *The Gentleman's Magazine* 15/9/1823, an elderly gentleman called Mr M Green reminisced: "The projected demolition of London Bridge recalls to my mind the introductory lines of an old Ballad which more than 70 years ago I heard plaintively warbled by a lady who was born in the Reign of Charles II and who lived until nearly the end of that of George II." The ballad he remembered is more or less the rhyme as set down in *Tommy Thumb's Pretty Song Book*.

He remembered the first line as "London Bridge is broken down". This is how it was still being listed in *Blackwood's Magazine* in 1821. The words 'falling down' may have first appeared a bit later. The Opies in *The Singing Game* (1985) mention "a fanciful" version of the song ('London Bridge is falling down, Dan's sister and Lady Anne) as being "remembered from childhood in the vicinity of Glasgow c1855".

Patricia Pierce believed the rhyme was very old dating back to the time when London Bridge was a timber bridge and then later the rhyme was revamped and updated to commemorate another bridge disaster.

In 1014 the old wooden bridge was destroyed in the Battle of Southwark. King Olaf II of Norway was fighting alongside King Ethelred (the one who was nicknamed 'the Unready') and Ethelred had paid him handsomely for his support. The idea was to stop the Vikings getting access to the City of London. After some forays Olaf decided to attach his boats to the piers of the bridge and, helped by the tide, pulled it down. His victory was celebrated by the Icelandic historian Snorri Sturluson in a collection of sagas about the victorious Olaf called *Heimskringla* written around 1230. This was translated by the 19th century writer Samuel Laing in 1844. Alice Gomme first drew the public's attention to Laing's translation which started:

> *London Bridge is broken down.*
> *Gold is won, and bright renown.*

This sounded like too much of a coincidence, wrote Lady Gomme, to be an "accidental parallel". For her the London Bridge disaster of 1014 was the origin of the rhyme. But this is discounted by scholars.

Samuel Laing was born in 1780 – 55 years after *Namby Pamby* when the rhyme was well-known. In 1930 the Norse scholar Margaret Ashdown published a study of documents relating to the reign of Ethelred the

Unready. In it she wrote that Laing's translation of Ottar the Black's *Hofuðlausn* "has a spirited and exceedingly free rendering of this stanza beginning 'London Bridge is broken down'". She added: "It would seem that this somewhat misleading paraphrase of Ottar's verse has given colour to the suggestion that the old singing game is connected with the episode commemorated by Ottar. She translated these lines more prosaically as: "And further, O prover of the serpent of Ygg's storms, valiant in war, you broke down London's bridge."

John Clark, then Honorary Reader at University College London's Institute of Archaeology, quoted above, pointed out in the *London Archaeologist* magazine (2002) that Samuel Laing's translation was never intended to be a literal one. His unintentionally misleading paraphrase, published in 1844, could not have influenced a song known from at least the 17th century. Clark went on to ask: "Is it then just 'an accidental parallel', as Mrs Gomme wondered? Probably not. It is surely most likely that Laing, intent on translating into resounding English couplets the obscurities of skaldic verse, and faced with a reference to Olaf 'breaking down' London Bridge, found inspiration in a rhyme that was as well known to him as it was to Mrs Gomme." … There is *no* other connection between the words of Ottar's verse and the rhyme first recorded in the 17th century."

If the London Bridge rhyme is not therefore about the Vikings it knocks out the earliest 'My Fair Lady' candidate - the Virgin Mary. This was based on the theory that the Vikings failed to take the city because as many at the time believed it was protected by the Virgin, especially as it took place on September 8th – her birthday.

If the poem isn't about sacrificial rites then another theory that the fair lady might have been a noblewoman called Lady Leigh falls apart. She was a member of the family that owned Stoneleigh Park in Warwickshire from 1561-1990. A family document contained a report of human sacrifice beneath the estate.

Dancing over Lady Lee? This is definitely a good clue from *Namby Pamby*. In the *Gentleman's Magazine,* Mr Green suggested: "It probably originated in some accident that happened to the Old Bridge. The 'Lady Lea' evidently refers to the river of that name, the favourite haunt of Isaac Walton, which, after fertilising the counties of Hertfordshire, Essex, and Middlesex, glides into the Thames." But how can a gay lady dance on a river?

If, as seems likely, Lady Lee is the River Lea (sometimes known as Lee), one of the largest rivers feeding into the Thames, then the 'gay or fair lady' could have been Queen Matilda of Scotland, the wife of Henry I who was responsible for building Bow Bridge, a bridge across the River Lea at Bow Interchange between 1100 and 1118. According to the historian Alison Weir: "Having been almost drowned – or at least 'well-washed' – riding across the River Lea at Stratford, east of London, she [Matilda] erected a 'beautiful bridge' there with stone arches and a chapel …." The like had never before been seen in England. And because of the bridge's bow-shaped arches the town became known as 'Stratford-Le-Bow'.

Although Alison Weir did not link Matilda to the fair lady I found one writer of history books who has. Erin Lawless in 2019 included Queen Matilda, who was called Edith at birth, in *Forgotten Royal Women*. She ended the chapter on her as follows: "One place where Edith/Matilda is not forgotten is in the words to the traditional nursery rhyme, *London Bridge is Falling Down*; legend has it that due to her proclivity for building bridges over tributaries to the Thames, she is the 'fair lady' referred to at the end of every verse."

Linda Alchin believed that the 'gay ladye' could have been Anne Boleyn and the rhyme was a metaphor of her rise and fall. This was because one of her childhood friends was called Lady Margaret Lee. She was one of the ladies-in-waiting allowed to stay with the unfortunate queen in the Tower until her execution and attended her on the scaffold.

Neither of these two royal ladies was involved in any disastrous event at London Bridge. The pages of *The Chronicles of London Bridge* show a very comprehensive time chart of the main events in the bridge's history. All were impeccably sourced from diaries and other documents kept by various people at the time. I have extrapolated from this the main disasters. One lady and one event (which I have marked in bold type) jumps out from this list and is supported by the line: "Dance over my Lady Lee."

	London Bridge time-line
	Courtesy of the index to Chronicles of London Bridge (1827)
1014	Battle of Southwark pulled down by Olaf of Norway.
1091	Massive whirlwind and flood washes bridge away completely.
1135/6	Old wooden bridge destroyed by fire.
1176	Stone bridge replaces old wooden structure and is completed in 1209. It has 19 arches. Chapel built dedicated to St Thomas Becket. Houses and shops were built on the bridge soon after its construction.
1212	Fire destroys southern end of bridge. 3000 people killed and drowned in boats trying to escape.
1269	Henry III grants his wife Eleanor custody of the bridge. But she allows it to fall into disrepair.
1282	Five arches of the bridge collapse because of pressure of ice. The Thames is frozen allowing crossings between Westminster and Lambeth. Edward I institutes a toll to raise money for repairs.
1426	Bridge reconstructed. Tower at north end repaired and drawbridge replaced so that ships can pass to Queenhithe.
1437	Southern end of London Bridge gives way and the tower collapses taking two arches with it.
1633	Fire breaks out at northern end of bridge. Over one third of the houses at northern end destroyed. Southern bridge survives.
1666	Bridge survives great fire of London because there are still gaps at its northern end according to Richard Thomson.
1758	Fatal fire on temporary bridge. Many of the houses in the bridge's centre destroyed.
1831	*New bridge built made of steel.*

If Lady Lee is a river, then you can dance over it only when it's frozen. That happened in 1281/82. John Stow the chronicler reported it in his *Annals* as edited by Howes of London in 1631: "From this Christmas till the Purification of Our Lady, there was such a frost and snow, as no man living could remember the like. Where through, five arches of London Bridge, and all Rochester Bridge, were borne downe and carried away by the streame; and the like hapned to many bridges in England. And, not long after, men passed over the Thames, between Westminster and Lambeth.....dry-shod."

Patricia Pierce explained how the unpopular Queen Eleanor of Provence, beautiful and greedy, was granted custody of the bridge by her husband Henry III in 1269. Six years earlier her barge had been cursed and pelted with eggs, stones and mud by the local people when she had tried to escape from the Tower of London during Henry's war with Simon de Montfort. Patricia Pierce writes: "The City-chosen wardens were replaced by others of her choosing who collected the rents and assets but spent nothing whatever on repairs."

Queen Eleanor resigned the custodianship of the bridge in September 1270 but according to the website *historyoflondon.com*: "Eleanor kept the income from the bridge for herself, starving it of funds needed for repairs. After Henry's death the citizens complained to Edward I that his mother was neglecting maintenance work. He passed responsibility for the bridge back to the City and issued an appeal for funds, stating that the Bridge of London is in so ruinous condition that not only the sudden fall of the bridge, but "also the destruction of innumerable people dwelling upon it, may suddenly be feared."

His appeal failed to save the bridge. It was in no position to withstand the prolonged severe frost of late 1281 and early 1282. Almost one quarter of the bridge was destroyed. And according to Patricia Pierce: "With this destruction by ice of almost one-quarter of Old London Bridge, the song of the *Olaf Sagas* was easily adapted in the late thirteenth century – perhaps very much earlier, back in the days of the timber bridges – to become a popular nursery rhyme."

Eleanor of Provence was so beautiful in her youth that she was called my fair lady. According to Agnes Strickland in her history of the queens of England: "She was married when she was only 14-years-old and became the most unpopular queen that ever reigned over the English court. She was so beautiful as to be called *La Belle*, but her judgement was too immature to stand all the adulation she received without being spoiled by it."

Very few biographies of this fair queen have been written since. But I enjoyed a sympathetic historical novel by the Canadian author J.P. Reedman which was published in 2016. It was called: *MY FAIR LADY: A Story of Eleanor of Provence, Henry III's Lost Queen*. On its first page is the nursery rhyme which explains the book's title.

CHAPTER EIGHT
MARY HAD A LITTLE LAMB
Fundraiser and fake

Mary had a little lamb,
Its fleece was white as snow;
And everywhere that Mary went
The lamb was sure to go.

It followed her to school one day,
Which was against the rule;
It made the children laugh and play
To see a lamb at school.

And so the teacher turned it out,
But still it lingered near,
And waited patiently about
Till Mary did appear.

. . . .

And then he ran to her, and laid
His head upon her arm,
As if he said, "I'm not afraid,
You'll keep me from all harm."

'What makes the lamb love Mary so?'
The eager children cry:
'O, Mary loves the lamb, you know.'
The teacher did reply.

'And you, each gentle animal
To you for life, may bind
And make it follow at your call
If you are always kind'.

Mary, had a little Lamb and its next three lines were rated by the distinguished 20th Century English literary critic F.R. Leavis as the most famous verse in the English language.

The four lines were chosen in 1877 by the American father of modern innovation, Thomas Alva Edison, as the most appropriate way of announcing one of his most famous inventions: the cylinder phonograph. He recited them into this machine with a mouthpiece and a recording needle, the precursor of both the tape-recorder and the gramophone, and was delighted and amazed when the machine repeated the lines back. But who wrote those lines? This is one of the most intriguing disputes in nursery rhyme history.

Just one year before Edison unveiled his famous phonograph the poem had been used widely in a fund-raising campaign to save one of the most historic buildings in Boston, USA, from destruction. This was in fact the Old South Meeting House, a Congregational church in the downtown area of the city.

The old church, built by the Puritans in 1729, was the largest meeting place in Boston. Five thousand angry Bostonians gathered there on December 16[th]1773, before they surged onto the docks, hurled tea-chests into the sea and so started the Boston Tea Party - the famous event which led to the American War of Independence.

In 1876 the renowned meeting hall was in desperate straits. It had been sold for demolition. The clock had been ripped off its imposing front entrance tower. The lead was being taken off the roofs and the copper was vanishing from its once dominating 180-feet-tall steeple. It was summer and the wealthy residents of Boston had deserted the city for the cooler hills or the seaside. The new owners gave the remaining business fraternity of Boston only two months in which to raise $420,000 to buy back the land on which the building stood.

Under the slogan: 'Shall the Old South be Saved?' the preservationists who included the poet Henry Wadsworth Longfellow, the *Little Women* author Louisa May Alcott, the essayist Ralph Waldo Emerson, the anti-slavery advocate Wendell Phillips and the jurist Oliver Wendell Holmes Junior, set to work.

They were helped by a group of determined ladies in Boston. Among them was a widow, Mary Elizabeth Tyler (née Sawyer), a 70-year-old farmer's daughter who lived in Somerville near the threatened building. She was selling strands of wool from two old pairs of stockings. The wool strands were attached to cards, each with Mary's signature, which claimed to be knitted "from the first fleece sheared from Mary's Little Lamb".

The cards quickly raised 100 bucks, then another 100 bucks. The old lady attended fundraising events in Boston in which she talked to children about how she was the original Mary of the famous poem and the money rolled in. The meeting house was saved.

So who was this Mary who had the little lamb? She had suddenly emerged from oblivion to claim ownership of a famous animal which had been dead for nearly 57 years. Mary Sawyer came from a long-established Massachusetts family of millwrights, wheelwrights, water-power workers and carpenters, and grew up on a farm in Sterling. Early on a cold bleak March morning, in the week of her ninth birthday in 1815, she visited the barn with her father to find that two female lambs had just been born. One of them was half dead. Her father told her that the other should also be left to die. But she could not bear to do this. She covered this lamb in a warm blanket throughout the day and stayed up all night, eventually weaning her onto catnip tea.

The Sawyer story described how the lamb survived and lived in a cowshed as she preferred cows to sheep and would follow Mary everywhere. One morning Mary called out to her as she left for school. The lamb gleefully came running bleating towards her. Her younger brother Nat suggested that as a joke she should take her to school.

When they reached the school the teacher Miss Polly Kimball had not yet arrived and there were only a few children there. Mary took the lamb with her into the classroom and as the desks were old-fashioned wooden desks boarded round the bottom, she covered her with a blanket and placed her in the cavity under her seat. The lesson started but it was not long before Mary was called to the front of the class to recite something. But as she walked there was a clatter clatter on the floor and she recognised the pattering hoofs of her lamb. The teacher laughed outright, and all the children giggled. But Mary was mortified. She was so ashamed that she took her lamb out of the classroom and put her in a shed. That lunchtime she took her home and stayed away from school.

Later that day a young lad called John Roulstone visited the school. He was the nephew of the local vicar, the Rev Lemuel Capen. Mary explained later in a letter to a friend: "It was the custom then for students to prepare for college with a minister and for this purpose Mr Roulstone was studying with his uncle."

Mary Sawyer went on to say that John was much pleased by the incident of the lamb. The next day he rode across the fields on horseback to the little old school house and handed her a piece of paper on which he wrote the first three verses above the dotted line as shown at the beginning of this chapter.

The lamb became an ewe and had three lambs of her own. But when she was four years old on Thanksgiving Day 1819 she was gored to death by a not so friendly cow who lowered its horns and butted her. The sheep gave an agonizing bleat, and with blood streaming from her sides, came to Mary who took her in her lap while she passed away. She sheared off her wool and her mother knitted two pairs of stockings out of it.

Unfortunately John Roulstone did not long survive the sheep. He was obviously bright, passed into Harvard University but died aged only 17 in his first or 'fresher' year in 1822. History does not relate why he died so young. An affectionate tribute from his uncle published at his funeral testified to the fact that he loved children. He delighted in making them happy and devoted much of his leisure to their amusement and affection. But sadly it didn't mention anything about John writing poetry about a little lamb some five to seven years previously.

The old lady, now Mrs Tyler, had no idea how Roulstone's piece of paper, now lost, had come into print and become so famous. Her family could only assume that the renowned Bostonian writer, editor and activist Sarah Josepha Hale had included it in her *Poems for Our Children* which had been published in 1830 and added three more moralistic verses (the ones below the dotted line at the head of this chapter).

Later that year in September 1830 the poem had appeared in the *Juvenile Miscellany*, a bi-monthly children's magazine published in Boston, Massachusetts. Over it were the initials S J H. Nothing much more was heard about the poem for another 27 years until it appeared anonymously in Professor William Holmes McGuffey's *Second Reader*, a standard American school textbook in 1857. It then leapt to prominence.

By then Sarah Josepha Hale was an influential magazine editor and was well-known both as a poet, writer and campaigner. In 1833 she founded the Boston Seamen's Aid Society. She put the considerable weight of the ladies' magazine which she edited behind the campaign to raise funds to complete the Bunker Hill Monument in Boston in 1843. This monument celebrates one of the great battles of the American War of Independence. She was one of the first novelists to write about slavery in *Northwood: Or Life North and South* (1852). She was the leader of a successful campaign which won President Abraham Lincoln's support for the creation of Thanksgiving Day as America's national holiday in October 1863. To cap it all she was a single mother who brought up five children after her husband died when the eldest one was only seven.

Mrs Hale said she may have been inspired to write *Mary had a Little Lamb* by her own experiences when teaching at a school near her New Hampshire home. Sherbrooke Rogers, author of *Sarah Josepha Hale – A New England Pioneer* (1985), wrote: "It was at this small school that the incident involving 'Mary's Lamb' is reputed to have taken place. Sarah was surprised one morning to see one of her students, a girl named Mary, enter the classroom followed by her pet lamb. The visitor was far too distracting to be permitted to remain in the building and so Sarah 'turned her out.' The lamb stayed nearby till school was dismissed and then ran up to Mary looking for attention and protection. The other youngsters wanted to know why the lamb loved Mary so much and their teacher explained it was because Mary loved her pet. Then Sarah used the incident to get a moral across to the class."

When questioned about the identity of Mary and the lamb Mrs Hale would say that it was partly invented but that it was quite common for households to adopt lambs and the incident of a lamb following a girl to school had probably happened many times.

The Massachusetts town of Sterling has to this day a small copper statue of the woolly lamb with a plaque which attributes the opening verse to John Roulstone. Henry Ford, the father of the motor car, had no doubts that both Mrs Tyler and Mrs Hale were right. He bought the one-room Old School House in Sterling in 1927 and had the frame of the wooden building (belonging to Mary Sawyer's family) transported 21 miles to Sudbury.

Two bronze plaques on boulders in the school courtyard praised the genius of Sarah Hale who had written the second half of the poem. A book published by the Fords in 1928 analysed the rhyme and showed that it came in two separate halves – the first written simply by a child and the second - with the more sophisticated verses and a moral - by an adult.

The Fords maintained that Mrs Hale had never said she wrote the first half of the poem – it was only her relatives who claimed this after her death. The Mary Tyler (née Sawyer) story was outlined and was supported by letters, newspaper articles and testimonies from herself and other members of her family, and an *affidavit* supporting her claim to the lamb's ownership. Pictures of lambs throughout the book conjured up imagery of 'Roulstone's' three verses travelling across the countryside from farm to farm, from the Middlesex County in Massachusetts to the Sullivan County in New Hampshire.

There was a further claimant to the Little Lamb ownership. Mary Hughes was the daughter of a Welsh sheep farmer from Llangollen in Denbighshire. This Mary took her lamb to school and one of her sisters claimed to have written the famous poem about it. Mrs Hughes died in 1931 and the family had a relief of a lamb chipped into the head of her tombstone in Broadwater Cemetery, Worthing. The only problem was that Mary of Llangollen was born in 1842 – 12 years after the poem first appeared.

So who was right? The redoubtable dame of Thanksgiving Day or the old farmer's daughter, who was an active member of the Women's Christian Temperance Union? Neighbours and friends attested: "Mrs Tyler lived a most highly respected lady and died at the age of 83 in December 1889. No one who knew her character could doubt her truthfulness, no one who knew her mind could doubt her alertness of memory, and both these qualities have weight in considering the story of Mary and the lamb."

Henry Ford's promotion of John Roulstone as the true author of the poem eventually stung the Hale family into action. Horatio Hale, Sarah's son, an eminent ethnologist, signed a statement which appeared in the *Boston Transcript* (10/4/1889) about the authorship of the well-known poem in *Poems for Our Children*. He wrote: "The book – which is now before me – comprises only twenty-four duodecimo pages on a stiff paper cover. It is not a compilation, but an original work composed throughout by Mrs Hale."

Four days before she died on April 30 1879 the 90-year-old author herself was constrained to dictate to her daughter Frances a letter to a Miss Brown which began: "The poem *Mary Had a Little Lamb* I wrote early in the year 1830 at the request of Mr Lowell Mason who desired me to write some poems for children to be set to music."

Sandra Sonnichsen, Volunteer Archivist of the Sarah J Hale Collection Library, New Hampshire, is scathing about Henry Ford's 'little book'. In an article written for the Richards Free Library, Newport, USA in 2016, she returned somewhat wearily to the fray and said *Mary had a Little Lamb* was a simple poem published with a clear authorship – Sarah J Hale, who hated plagiarism.

She said Henry Ford might have 200 documents to prove his point but he provided no evidence that the poem was written for Mary Tyler née Sawyer. The supposed author was dead, his uncle the minister was dead, there was no testimony from the teacher. Why did Mrs Sawyer wait until 1876 to make her claim and was it anything to do with raising money for a treasured old building?

Ms Sonnichsen said the inclusion of a different moralistic tone in the latter half of the poem was a common format for children's poems at the time. As for the idea that the poem was wafted across the countryside she pointed out that the distance for those travelling in those days was some 90 miles and added drily: "Henry had not yet invented the automobile, so the distance was considerable." There was no mention that could be found of Roulstone's 'poem' in any letter or newspaper article. She concluded: "Ford turned an admirable old woman's fond memory into a vigorous promotional scheme without a thought for any historical fact."

Albert Jack is also sceptical that Mary Sawyer was the original owner of the 'little lamb'. In the first place he wondered in *Pop Goes the Weasel* (2008) if the lamb was so special to Mary why it didn't have a name?

Albert Jack might have mentioned one further point which concerns me: the age of Roulstone at the time the poem was written. He died aged 17 in February 1822.

The lamb was born in March 1815 when Roulstone would have been only 10. This lamb must have been small to fit beneath the desk. And a lamb soon becomes a sheep within a year. Although the Ford book tried to make Roulstone 12 (by quoting a note by one Francis Sawyer) he was more likely to have been 10 or 11 at most. What was he doing being prepared for Harvard University before his early teens and above all riding around the countryside on a horse when he should have been at school?

But the proof in the rhyme's authorship could lie in the gender of the lamb:

And then he ran to her, and laid
His head upon her arm,

Mrs Sawyer's lamb was clearly female. The last three verses (as published in 1830) make it clear (see start of this chapter) as did the whole poem originally that Sarah Hale's lamb was in fact a young ram – a male!

I have to conclude that Mrs Sawyer was a good fundraiser but she had a fanciful memory.

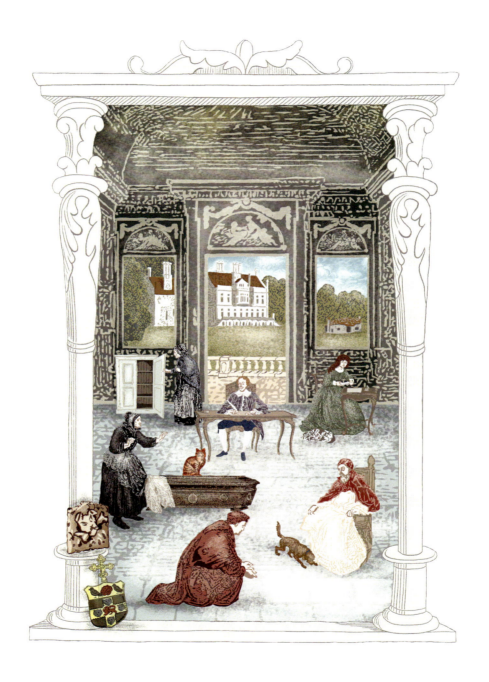

CHAPTER NINE

OLD MOTHER HUBBARD

Old Mother Wolsey?

> Old Mother Hubbard (Cardinal Wolsey)
> Went to the cupboard (the Church at Rome)
> To fetch the poor doggie (Henry VIII) a bone (the divorce scroll)
> When she got there, the cupboard was bare (the Pope said no)
> And the poor doggie had none (Henry VIII didn't get his divorce).

The identity of Old Mother Hubbard seems so cut and dried when explained like this by Sandy Leong in *Warts & All* (2018). She and other nursery rhyme detectives thought *Old Mother Hubbard* was a skit on Cardinal Thomas Wolsey, Henry VIII's Chief Minister, who failed to persuade the pope to agree to the king's decision to divorce his first wife Catherine of Aragon so that he could marry Anne Boleyn.

Wolsey is known to have had a dog. Perhaps he was a hungry dog as some jokingly say the animal caused the Reformation! In a 1570 edition of John Foxe's *Acts and Monuments* also known as *Foxes Book of Martyrs,* the following passage appeared: "For he [*Wolsey*] having there a great spaniel which came out of England with him, stood directly between the earl and the bishop of Rome, when the said bishop had advanced forth his foot to be kissed. Now whether the spaniel perceived the bishop's foot of another nature than it ought to be, and so taking it to be some kind of repast – or whether it was the will of God to show some token by a dog unto the bishop of his inordinate pride, that his feet were more meet to be bitten of dogs …….when the bishop extended his foot to be kissed ……went directly to the pope's feet, and not only kissed the same unmannerly with his mouth, but, as some plainly reported and affirmed, took fast with his mouth the great toe of the pope, so that in haste he pulled in his glorious feet from the spaniel."

The idea of Old Mother Thomas Wolsey was first proposed by our old friend Katherine Elwes Thomas in *The Real Personages of Mother Goose* (1930). And yet again her logic is not impeccable. Her explanation was based on reading Thomas Churchyard's *The Tragedy of Thomas Wolsey*. The relevant lines she quoted in *The Tragedy* were:

> *Then was I led towards Court like*
> *Dog in string,*

and

> *To fawning dogs sometimes I gave a bone,*
> *And flung some scraps to such as nothing had.*

According to her the connection between Hubbard and Wolsey may have been inspired by a 'wretched figure' above the cardinal's coat of arms in Christ Church College Cathedral, Oxford, which features a dog gnawing a bone! She found a reference to a figure above the windows in the cathedral in George Howard's *Life of Cardinal Wolsey* (1824). Although this clue does not remotely prove beyond all reasonable doubt that Cardinal Wolsey was Mother Hubbard, she was at least correct about the figure's existence. Nearly 200 years later in February 2023 the 576 ornamental carvings or 'bosses' in the cathedral ceiling were being cleaned. And this one, with the dog gnawing the bone, was one of the first to be discovered.

So, we must start, as we have with other rhymes in this book, with how the rhyme first saw the light of day. The 14-verse *Comical Adventures of Old Mother Hubbard and her Dog* was written by Sarah Catherine Martin, a one-time girlfriend of the future King William IV (of England). It was a spectacular success when it was first published by John Harris as a toy book (the name given to illustrated children's books) on 1st June 1805. Ten thousand copies were distributed in a few months. Pirated copies and editions soared. Old Mother Hubbard's adventures have been printed and reprinted and translated all over the world including China and Russia, and the dog's antics acted out in pantomimes ever since.

At the time many thought the rhyme was poking fun at a contemporary politician and that was partly why it might have been so successful. But no one knew who the politician might be. And the author wasn't saying. But experts agree that similar verses of the rhyme are older than 1805. They were well known and had been published before Sarah Martin wrote her *Comical Adventures*. For example, her third verse went as follows:

She went to the undertakers
To buy him a coffin;
But when she came back
The poor dog was laughing

A comic ballad based on *Old Dame Trot and Her Comical Cat* published by T. Evans in 1803 had a similar title and verses. For example one went:

She went to the undertakers
For a coffin and Shroud
When she came back,
Puss sat up and mewed

James Orchard Halliwell, the 19th century collector of nursery rhymes and an expert on Shakespeare, considered that the first three verses were older than the rest because of the rhyme of 'Coffin' with 'laughing'. 'Loffe' is an old English word for 'laugh' which Shakespeare uses in *A Midsummer Night's Dream* (Act 2 sc 1). So the verse would have ended 'loffing'.

It seems that although Sarah Martin did not invent Mother Hubbard she created the dog by rewriting the first three verses and adding a further eleven using rhymes and ideas from contemporary rhymes.

Further evidence that Mrs Hubbard was a well-known figure long before 1805 is contained in a review of Miss Martin's toybook (a name used to describe illustrated children's books in the 19th century) which appeared in *The Guardian of Education* in September 1805. It was edited by Sarah Trimmer, the educationalist, children's author and Sunday school advocate. She commented that the poetry in this little book was of "ancient date" and stories about Mrs Hubbard were current when she was young in the 1740s. She wrote: "We can recollect, at this distance of time, that in our infant days the story of this renowned woman, though full of inconsistencies we confess, afforded us much entertainment."

Around 1590 Edmund Spenser composed a satirical beast fable in which some of the animals could have been political figures. It was called 'Prosopopoia or Mother Hubberd's Tale'. The poem is the nearest Spenser got to Chaucer's *Canterbury Tales* and was about a sick bedridden poet who had visitors to entertain him with stories. But only the best story was related in the long poem:

> *Amongst the rest, a good old woman was,*
> *Hight [called] Mother Hubberd, who did farre surpas*
> *The rest in honest mirth, that seem'd her well:*
> *She when her turne was come her tale to tell,*
> *Tolde of a strange aduenture, that betided*
> *Betwixt the Fox and th' Ape by him misguided;*

This poem which could have been about the courting of Queen Elizabeth by the Duc d'Alençon (the ape) had nothing to do with Cardinal Wolsey.

Lina Eckenstein in her book on comparative nursery rhymes (1906) pointed out that the name of Mother Hubburd or Hubbard was familiar long before the publication of the dame and her dog by Sarah Martin. Father Hubbard figured in nursery lore. He also conveniently rhymes with cupboard as was shown by this rhyme published in 1887 in the scholarly journal *Notes & Queries*. It had been sent in by a reader who had learnt it from his old nurse:

> *What's in the cupboard? Says Mr Hubbard;*
> *A knuckle of veal, says Mr Beal;*

In 2012 Lesley Jane Delaney, a PhD student at University College London, wrote a thesis on *Key developments in the Nursery Reading Market (1783-1900)*. In it she wrote: "The title 'Mother' was typically used to refer to old women of the lower classes, and a similar character is referred to in Edmund Spenser's satire. Martin was probably familiar with the connotations of the character, as her drawings feature

Mother Hubbard as a portly country dame……. Martin's carnivalesque rhyme turns the world topsy-turvy with its anthropomorphised dog, but the humour indicates to the reader that this is not a story to be taken seriously; it is simply a nonsense rhyme about a dog that can sing and dance, read and write."

Old Mother Hubbard might have been written on the spur of the moment. The Baring-Goulds, in their extensive 1962 nursery rhyme collection *The Annotated Mother Goose*, relate how in 1804 Sarah was visiting Kitley House in Yealmpton, near Plymouth in South Devon, the home of her future brother-in-law, John Pollexfen Bastard, MP for Devonshire. "One day she was chattering away in her usual fashion while her host was trying to write a letter. Annoyed he told her to run away and write something herself – 'one of your stupid little rhymes', was the way he put it."

And Sarah bore no ill-will to her host. For in 1806 another edition of the booklet was dedicated to J.B. Esq by "his humble servant SCM" with the tongue-in-the-cheek message "at whose suggestion and at whose House these noble sketches were designed". The book was illustrated with 15 elegant engravings on copper plate.

According to an old tradition in the Bastard family (mentioned by the Opies in 1951) an inscription in their original copy of *The Comical Adventures* contained information that Mrs Hubbard was the housekeeper at Kitley. Although I could not find a copy of this edition the Bastard family still believe this was how the rhyme originated.

The family, whose forebears came over with William the Conqueror, still own Kitley House and its 600-acre estate. Sarah Hardy, wife of the present proprietor, sent me a copy of an article from the magazine *Country Life* dated 7th October 1939 by its editor, Christopher Hussey, the distinguished architectural historian. He described how John Bastard had married "secondly a Miss Martin, whose sister Sarah lived in the house and wrote the original 'Mother Hubbard' rhymes for her step-nieces and nephews." He added: "Mother Hubbard is believed to have been housekeeper at Kitley."

Sarah also sent me a photo of a souvenir edition of the Yealmpton Playes Fayre programme for an event which was held at Kitley on June 29th 1927. This reprinted the verses as they appeared in the original presentation copy of the rhyme and proclaimed boldly that: "Mother Hubbard was the housekeeper at Kitley at that time."

Kitley House was a luxury hotel until (as a result of the pandemic) it had to close in July 2020. Before it closed a historical guide to the 16th century home on its website claimed that 'Mrs Hubbard' was a resident housekeeper and her cupboard is "located in the basement area where she had her sitting room".

She may have also lived somewhere else. The Bastard family used to run a tea-shop in nearby Market Street. It is called 'Mother Hubbard's Cottage' and is described on the website *Britain Express* as a beautiful example of a thatched Tudor hall house. For some years they have rented it out and as Oliver Tearle informed his readers in *Britain by the Book* (2017): "In Yealmpton you can visit Mother Hubbard's Cottage and find the cupboards anything but bare. Indeed there's plenty of food on offer: it's now a Chinese takeaway and restaurant."

CHAPTER TEN

POP GOES THE WEASEL

The dance that went crazy

Half a pound of tuppeny rice,
Half a pound of treacle,
That's the way the money goes,
Pop! goes the weasel!

King James I, lampooned as the 'Wisest Fool in Christendom', was, according to the Opies, also known as the 'Weasel'. This was because of his thin sharp features and red hair. 'Rice' was a slang term for potassium nitrate and 'treacle' was a slang name for charcoal. Gunpowder, invented by Chinese alchemists in the ninth century, was originally made from sulphur, charcoal and potassium nitrate and can go 'pop'. Put all these clues together and this rhyme could have originated with a famous plot by Guy Fawkes and his band of conspirators to blow up James I of England (also James VI of Scotland).

This was one explanation for the origin of *Pop Goes the Weasel* put forward by the Opies in their 1985 book *The Singing Game*. But they didn't go into it in any more detail and we do know from history that the weasel didn't go 'pop' on November 5th 1605 as the Gunpowder Plot failed.

However, 250 or so years later the Scottish king might unwittingly have been responsible for *Pop goes the Weasel*. Seven generations directly down the royal line from James I came Queen Victoria. Her love of country dancing in the years before her beloved Albert died (1861) could have been responsible for bringing *Pop Goes the Weasel* to prominence in England. In 1854 the musical publishers Boosey & Sons advertised 'the new country dance' and claimed that "it had been introduced by Her Majesty Queen Victoria".

The earliest recording of the song is in a sheet of music for a polka dance by W. H. Montgomery which was acquired by the British Library on 14th March

1853. It was sold by D'Almaine & Co of 20 Soho Square, London, along with Montgomery's "new Buckingham Palace Waltzes". It had a tune very similar to the one used today but only included the one line at the end: 'Pop Goes the Weasel'. There was nothing about the rice or the treacle or 'the way the money goes'.

By then *Pop Goes the Weasel* was sufficiently well-known for it to be the name of a boat which was reported in The *Newcastle Courant* (18/6/1852) as taking part in the Durham Regatta. This was an annual procession of flotillas from Prebends Bridge to Old Durham Beck, begun 18 years previously to celebrate the victory at Waterloo.

Six months later *The Suffolk Chronicle* reported an Ipswich ball on 13th December 1852 where *Pop Goes the Weasel* had been "one of the most inspiring dances which can well be imagined". Twelve days later, on Christmas Day, the *Birmingham Journal* advertised lessons to learn the steps of a "highly fashionable dance, recently introduced at her Majesty's and the Nobility's private soirées". On December 29th that year *The Times Supplement* carried an advertisement for a one shilling handbook on the latest fashionable dances containing the sheet music and steps of the new dance which "had been such a success at the Court balls".

This handbook made it clear that *Pop goes the Weasel* was "an old and very animated dance that had lately been revived among the higher classes of society". The dance music in the handbook also contained only the last line. M. Eugène Coulon, who wrote it, was a teacher of dancing credited with introducing several dances to England including the polka and the mazurka. Born in Paris, the son of a famous dance professor, he had first moved to Holland where he taught the children of the Prince of Orange. In 1837 he went on to London where the preface to the handbook said: "He worked for some families of the highest rank in England."

At some point the dance crossed to the United States because a sheet of music dated 1853 (with only the weasel line) is available at the Library of Congress in Washington DC. US newspapers called it: "the latest English dance".

That year the song was all the rage in London's theatreland. Royal Holloway College, University of London, has a list of plays licensed in London in 1853. One for a performance at the Theatre Royal, Haymarket on 5 February referred to: "*Pop goes the Weasel* as now danced at nearly all the theatres in the metropolis". The National Standard Theatre in Shoreditch was given a licence for a performance of *Pop goes* the Weasel, or, The adventures of the weasel family*, described as 'a farce in one act' on May 2nd. A burletta (theatrical piece with music in one act) called *Pop goes the Weasel or The devil's dance* was given a licence for a performance at the Pavilion Theatre in Whitechapel Road on May 6th. *Pop Goes the Weasel* was one of the songs in the pantomimes at the Theatre Royal Drury Lane on December 19th and at the Britannia Saloon in Hoxton on Boxing Day.

Soon according to the Opies "everyone was fitting words to the catchy ubiquitous tune". *The Concise Oxford Dictionary of Quotations* has the traditional City verse of the song being composed by W.R. Mandale in 1853 and attributed the words to Charles Twiggs. Another Charles, Charles Sloman, comic entertainer, singer and songwriter, was credited by David Conway, the Hebrew scholar of *Jewry in Music* (2011), with being the original composer. And the Opies quoted his opening lines as follows:

> *Something new starts every day,*
> *Pop goes the weasel!*

Pop goes the Weasel has often been thought to be a coded-rhyming cockney slang lament for the working classes of Hackney in London's East End. They spent too much money at the boozer so they had to pawn their coats to get funds for basic foods like rice and treacle.

The best-known second 'City Road' verse (see below) must have already been in circulation when James Robinson Planché, the dramatist and theatrical costume expert, quoted it in his *Easter Extravaganza* at the Theatre Royal's New Haymarket Spring Meeting. This is listed in *The Extravaganzas of J.R. Planché* and took place on Easter Monday April 9th 1855. Many of the London theatre impresarios attended and were ceremoniously introduced. Among them was Benjamin Conquest, who in 1851 had acquired the Eagle Tavern in Shepherdess Walk off City Road, Hackney, a former pub which had closed in 1825. It then had a theatre attached called the Grecian Saloon. Mr Conquest was represented by a performer in an eagle costume who sang:

> *I'm the Bird of Conquest - made*
> *First by Romans famous.*

Though 'Grecian' my Saloon was named,
By some ignoramus.
Up and down the City Road,
In and out the Eagle
That's the way my money comes
Pop goes the weasel!

'Comes' in the fifth line replaces 'goes' to show that this was where the money was going - into the pockets of the Eagle's owners. It was then a music hall and a popular rendezvous for singing and Saturday night drinking and many other activities including wrestling, spectacular shows and operas with nightly audiences of up to 6,000. By that time 'weasel and stoat' was well-known rhyming slang for 'coat' and 'pop' was slang for pawn (*Oxford English Dictionary*).

By 1855 the nursery rhyme had become a very well-known street song played on barrel organs. The 44th *Annual Report of the National Society for Promoting the Education of the Poor in the Principles of the Established Church throughout England and Wales* contained correspondence with two different views about *Pop goes the Weasel*. A Mr Percival Prosser said that the song was a "contagious and pestilent harmony" and warned that children could be "deeply impressed with the sin of intemperance" as a result. The song was: "So thoroughly debasing in its character that almost every species of ribaldry and low wit has been reduced into rhyme to suit it."

Maria Theresa, a teacher, replied: "Whenever one of those nuisances was heard grinding the tune, the children would in the playground begin singing and dancing to the original senseless words. They still sing and dance but to better words. In the schoolroom too I find the song to great advantage. Instead of entirely stopping (for when an organ is playing close to an infant school no work will be done), we stop for a moment, sing the song of which your correspondent complains and again resume our lessons without the inattention which is the common result of listening to an organ."

In 1856, according to the *Londonist* website (18/1/2019) a correspondent to the Conservative *Morning Post* complained: "Sir, For many months everybody has been bored with the eternal grindings of this ditty on the street."

By then the traditional third verse to the tune had been added as follows:

Every night when I go out,
The monkey's on the table,
Take a stick and knock it off,
Pop! goes the weasel.

The 'monkey', which might well have been associated with the animal that commonly accompanied the organ-grinder, has been interpreted here as an old sailor's word for a tankard and a 'stick' was used to measure the amount of liquid left in a bottle or a shot of it. And 'knock it off' means 'knock the alcohol back'.

Those who support the theory that the rhyme is about weavers in Spitalfields, London, quote another verse:

A penny for a spool of thread,
Another for a needle,
That's the way the money goes
Pop goes the weasel.

It seems very likely that the dance preceded the rhyme as it was said to be not a new dance but a revival of an old one. We know also that the original dance music only had the 'pop goes the weasel' line. If any of the other lines had been in existence, they would surely have been included on that sheet in the dance handbooks and on the early sheets that crossed the Atlantic.

The dance was also a game. The Opies recorded the words of an 11-year-old girl from Stirling describing it in 1961: "You make several circles of three or four. Each circle has a weasel in the middle and there is an extra weasel outside. You dance round singing the song and when it comes to 'Pop Goes the Weasel' most run into the middle of a different ring and the old weasel must try to get inside one before it is filled. It is a bit like Musical Chairs."

Pop goes the weasel describes the end of a highly popular dance and the rest of the words are probably nonsense. The best evidence for this is from the composer of the song himself. The Opies ended their chapter on the song in *The Singing Game* by observing that even at the height of the dance craze in the 1850s no one seemed to have known what the song meant – not even one of the earliest composers. W.R. Mandale, they said, had asked everyone he had met what it meant and concluded:

> *I'm still as wise as e'er I was*
> *As full's an empty pea-shell*
> *In as far as the true history goes*
> *Of 'Pop goes the weasel'.*

CHAPTER ELEVEN

RIDE A COCK HORSE

The Princess and the statue

Ride a cock horse to Banbury Cross,
To see an old woman [or a fine lady] on a white horse;
With rings on her fingers and bells on her toes,
She shall have music wherever she goes.

Did Queen Elizabeth I ever go on a triumphal visit to Banbury town? Yes she did according to Katherine Elwes Thomas. Good Queen Bess's ride through the Oxfordshire town was the inspiration for not just this nursery rhyme but for her book *The Real Personages of Mother Goose* (1930).

Katherine wrote "It had its inception in a never-to-be-forgotten incident of my childhood, when, standing beside my mother as she sang, 'ride a cock horse to Banbury Cross', she smilingly remarked, 'The old woman on the white horse was Queen Elizabeth.' This comment made with the certainty of one who repeats a well-known fact convinces me that somewhere in England and the Colonies there must have existed a traditional knowledge of the original import of all these delightful rhymes."

I had the greatest fun exploring the 'import' of this rhyme. Those four lines at the top of this chapter contain many mysteries and alternative theories. Starting with the word 'cock horse' the *Oxford English Dictionary* has six definitions for the animal. Then there were three crosses in Banbury in the Middle Ages as well as an ancient crossing outside the Oxfordshire town. There are seven possible contenders for the fine or old lady who might have ridden on a white or black or grey horse because as the rhyme evolved so did the colour of the horse and the age of its rider.

"Uncle, what is a cock-horse?' asked a little girl bouncing on the knee of a contributor to *Harper's Magazine* in 1882. The kindly uncle did a lot of research to come up with a picture of a *hippalectryon*, a 'horse cock' as named by the Greeks, represented on an ancient Etruscan vase, which he claimed was more than 2,500 years old. On the vase a handsome youth is riding a prancing animal, with the head and legs of a horse, and large wings and a fanned tail - half-horse and half-rooster or in other words 'half-cock!'

Not so long afterwards in 414 BC in *The Birds* the Greek playwright Aristophanes used the hybrid to describe either an upstart man who has risen from nowhere or an army general giving himself airs – or in other words 'cocky'. In this sense the word was used by the Elizabethan poet Christopher Marlowe, not long before he was killed in a tavern brawl, and published posthumously in his poem *Hero and Leander* (1598):

> *Our painted fools and cockhorse peasantry*
> *Still, still usurp, with long lives, love, and lust,*
> *The seats of Virtue, cutting short as dust.*

For a third meaning you need only to go to a little English village called Detling, a few miles northeast of Maidstone in Kent. Here on the Pilgrims' Way there has been a hostelry called The Cock Horse Inn since the 14th century. According to the latest updated version of the *Dover Kent Archives*: "The name is derived from the need to supply a cock horse to provide the necessary horsepower to get stagecoaches and heavy carts up a hill."

On January 2nd 1930 the *Sunday Times* printed answers from two of its readers to the question of what a cock horse was. Both said it meant the spare horse stationed at the foot of a steep hill to help coaches to ascend it. The rider was called 'a cok horse boy'. One of them, Mr W. Roger Rowlatt-Jones from Bournemouth, recalled: "It was a customary sight during the latter half of the eighteenth century for travellers to Banbury and Birmingham to observe a group of children clustered at the foot of Stanmore Hill to witness the be-ribboned and rosetted fifth horse attached to the coach. As the gaily caparisoned jockey flourished his gilt-staff the boys and girls would chant: 'Ride a cock-horse to Banbury Cross,' etc., and that nursery rhyme may have originated there."

A hobby horse – a toy stick with a horse's head at the end mentioned in a 14th century Welsh poem – is often called a cock horse. The word was also found in a translation of a Latin text by the diplomat and scholar, Thomas Elyot. He included it in *Image of Gouernance*: "The dotynge pleasure to se my litell sonne ryde on a cokhorse." I found it on page 95-96 in an edition, dated 1556, in the British Library. A character known as Eucolpius was discussing how sterility could deprive him of seeing his son having fun in the nursery and chattering.

This riding stick could also date back to antiquity: Robert Burton in his *Anatomy of Melancholy* (1621) described how even the grave Socrates (c470-399BC) could be 'merry by fits'. Burton described how the sage's famous pupil Xenophon, the writer and general, recalled how his master, the philosopher, 'would ride a cock-horse with his children' – *equitare in arudine longa* (to ride on a long rod).

Percy B. Green, author of *A History of Nursery Rhymes* (1899) noted that Agesilaus II, King of Sparta from c 400 to 360 BC, "in mere sport romped with his children, and delighted them by riding on a stick round the nursery, possibly singing [the rhyme] after the manner of many a modern rollicking nursery-loving father."

Fifthly, there has for centuries been a toddlers' game of riding a cock horse while bouncing on the foot of an adult. And the adults who have participated have included like Socrates the strictest of people. Herbert Gladstone, youngest son of William the famous Liberal prime minister, remembered: "We had teaspoonfuls of black coffee and rides on his foot slung over his knee while he sang 'Ride a cock horse to Banbury Cross'. … It was a daily treat."

Mr William Potts, editor and founder of the *Banbury Guardian,* had another meaning. In *Banbury Cross and the Rhyme* (1930) he explained how cockhorse could be used as an adverb. This use dated back to medieval times to describe two people riding 'a-cock-horse' with the knight in front and a lady behind him on a pillion (saddle). He cited James Orchard Halliwell's *Dictionary of Archaic and Provincial Words* (1852) which said it could be applied to two persons on the same horse.

'Banbury Cross?' Need it be a structure at all? Those who believed the rhyme dated back to an ancient pagan festival pointed to a prehistoric settlement to the south-west of the town at the crossing of two ancient ways: Salt Way, which stretched from Worcestershire to London, and Banbury Lane, part of the old Jurassic Way which joined the Humber to the Avon. The junction could have been the 'cross' in the rhyme. At the intersection there is an artificial Anglo-Saxon mound, 538 feet high, called Crouch Hill which was known as 'Cruge Hill' and this might have been Latinized to 'Crux' or 'Cross'.

The town of Banbury was originally known to have at least three crosses - the Bread Cross, the White Cross, and the High or Market Cross. In the 1966 edition of *Oxoniensia*, the annual journal of the Oxford Architectural and Historical Society, there is a 23-page article by Professor Paul D.A. Harvey, an historian and expert on medieval town maps. It was called: 'Where was Banbury Cross?'

He believed the one referred to in the nursery rhyme was the High Cross and it stood in the north-west of the marketplace in an area known as Cornhill. He was the first person to identify its proper position and to describe its destruction, according to the editor of the Banbury Historical Society magazine which has the wonderful title: *Cake and Cockhorse*.

Harvey's calculations were based on a description of the town by John Leland or Leyland, the Tudor poet and antiquarian. In his *Itinerary*, an account of his travels between 1535 and 1543, he wrote about Banbury: "The fayrest street of the towne lyethe by west and easte downe to the river of Charwelle. And at the weste part of this streat is a large area invironed with meatlye good buildings, havynge a goodlye crosse with many degrees [steps] about it. In this area is kept every Thursday a very celebrate market."

A new cross was erected to commemorate the wedding of Queen Victoria's eldest daughter (Vicky) to the Prince of Prussia in 1858. It stands in the Horse Fair where Alfred Beesley, the renowned 19th century Banbury historian, and William Potts, thought it should be. Mistakenly, according to Professor Harvey, they had assumed the 'fayreste' street in the town must have been the High Street rather than Bridge Street. The replacement cross is, he calculated, a quarter of a mile away from where it should be.

So what happened to the ancient High Cross in the marketplace? It dated back to at least 1441 when it was mentioned twice in a Rent Roll (listing the town's properties) kept by the Bishop of Lincoln, whose diocese then encompassed Banbury. Alas, it was too ornate to survive.

In the 17th century Banbury began to be renowned for being a hotbed for Puritan zeal. Ben Jonson in his play *Bartholomew Fair* (1614) used 'Banbury Man' as a synonym for 'Puritan' and described how a baker had to give up his trade for making Banbury cakes because they were used for 'profane feasts'.

Puritans went to extremes to keep the Sabbath holy as in this skit in *Barnabees Journal* (1638) by the poet Richard Brathwait:

> *To Banbery came I, O prophane one!*
> *Where I saw a Puritane one*
> *Hanging of his cat on Monday*
> *For killing of a mouse on Sunday.*

Records kept by the Society of Jesus contain a letter from a Rev. Anthony Rivers, a Jesuit priest, who wrote to a friend in Venice after the cross had been destroyed in 1600: "The inhabitants of Banbury being far gone in Puritanism, in a furious zeal tumultuously assailed the cross that stood in their marketplace and so defaced it that they scarcely left one stone upon another."

Matthew Knight, a mercer or cloth merchant, was watching in dismay from his nearby shop, when soon after dawn on July 26th 1600 he saw two stone masons hacking at the base of the cross. He told them to stop and went off to get help. But by the time he returned the two masons, cheered by five aldermen of the town and many in a crowd of about 100, destroyed the base with iron bars which they used as levers. As the cross toppled over one of the aldermen, Henry Shewell, cried out with a 'loude voyce and in a reioyeing manner': "God be thanked their god dagon is fallen downe to the ground ."

The five aldermen were later prosecuted for the damage in the Court of Star Chamber. The Court's records for 1604 contained a deposition by Matthew Knight who said that the cross was built of stone, surrounded by a flight of eight steps, 24 feet long and two feet wide, with a tall shaft emerging from a block of stone. On top of it was a cross and carvings which had "objects of superstitious veneration" carved by John Traford, of Grimsbury, who used to "take his hat off when he passed them".

It's likely that all three crosses were destroyed at about the same time by the Puritans. Sometime between 1618 and 1621 Bishop Richard Corbet, a metaphysical poet, visited Banbury and lamented in his poem *Iter Boreale*:

> *The crosses also, like old stumps of Trees,*
> *Or stooles for horsemen that have feeble knees*
> *Carry no heads above Ground.*

Now we come to the fine or old lady. The oldest surviving sighting of the 'fine lady' emerged in 1797 when the Rev. Baptist Noel Turner, a friend of Dr Samuel Johnson, included her in his version of the rhyme in *Infant Institutes* which he described as a "nurserical essay on the poetry, lyric and allegorical, of the earlier ages". The Rev Turner, according to the Opies, didn't appear to have a source book for his rhymes but relied on his memory for the wording of most of them. He remembered:

> *Hight-a-cock-horse to Banbury Cross,*
> *To see a fine lady upon a white horse;*

William Potts, editor of the *Banbury Guardian,* mentioned earlier in this chapter, put forward a rather simple theory that the fine lady on a white horse was an anonymous Queen of the May. He wasn't the first to do so as he mentioned a local artist, J. Hutchings, who had painted a large oil painting (56"x36") of a lady on a white horse surrounded by Morris dancers with Banbury Church in the background. The painter lived in Crouch Street in the town and enjoyed some fame as a painter after 1849. According to Benezit's *Dictionary of Artists* he exhibited his work in London from 1859-1893.

Mr Potts argued that the rhyme must have originated "when there was a Banbury Cross of which to sing" and it went back at least to the 16th century and probably very much further than that. He believed the rhyme contained a hidden piece of folklore: "The greatest religious festival among primitive peoples was that connected with the Earth Goddess which was held in the Spring of the year. The goddess was personified by a girl who in the earliest observances was presented as nude or decked with nature's covering of leaves and flowers.... It survived as a secular festival in our May Day observances, the dethroned Earth Goddess becoming the Queen of the May and the sacred tree the Maypole."

Cotswolds Info, the regularly updated website for tourists, has another pagan origin for the fine lady: "the Welsh horse goddess Rhiannon who features in the *Mabinogion* (a medieval collection of Middle Welsh stories). Another website, *Wiccaweb*, refers to the feast of Beltane celebrated on 30th April/1st May when fires would be lit to celebrate the light and described Rhiannon as "the goddess of the crossroads". It says: "At Beltane she was believed to ride to the cross of ley lines [straight lines connecting three or more prehistoric sites] where the power would be strongest, the cock (male) horse being her consort."

'Ride a cock horse to Coventry Cross to see what Emma can buy' appeared in a *Mother Goose* version of the rhyme published around 1850 and has led to the suggestion that the rhyme was about Lady Godiva and her famous naked ride through that city to protest against the taxes her husband was imposing. Albert Jack supported this as one possible theory and she's mentioned by other rhyme interpreters because she's one of the most celebrated of medieval female horse riders and her famous ride was reported to have been through Coventry.

Eunice Harradine described herself as a retired Banbury driving instructor and provider of education and learning in "438 different subcategories". In her *Banbury History*, revised 2005, on the internet she said that it was now generally accepted that the 'Fyne Lady' in question was a member of the Fiennes family. Celia Fiennes came from a well-connected dynasty that could trace its ancestry back to William of Wykeham, the bishop who founded Winchester College and New College, Oxford and now can progress it forward to today's actors Ralph and Joseph. Bishop William also owned Broughton Castle three miles south-west of Banbury. Celia would have known the town well as her brother, William Fiennes, was the third Viscount Saye and Sele. Between 1684 and about 1703 she rode on horseback all over the country "to regain her health", and made meticulous notes about her travels which were later published by her family.

Contributing to the *Sunday Times*'s discussion about the rhyme in 1930, a distant family descendant Lieutenant Colonel Fiennes W.E. Blake wrote on November 16th that the second line referred to the lady from Broughton Castle and should have read:

> *To see a Fiennes lady upon a white horse.*

On 2nd January 2006 there came a claim from New Zealand that the fine lady was none other than Lady Katherine Banbury, daughter of the Earl of Banbury and married to Lord Jonathan Banbury. This came from David Miller, a cousin of a New Zealand nurse called Amy Banbury. He said Amy distinctly recalled her grandfather remembering the white horse on which Lady Katherine rode and the bells which trimmed her velvet saddlecloth. This was in a long discussion about the rhyme on *mudcat.org* which continued into 2007.

Before I narrow down these suspects for the role of the fine lady let me go to the last part of the rhyme:

With rings on her fingers and bells on her toes
She shall have music wherever she goes.

The website *FashionologiaHistoriana* (14/12/2017) in an article on medieval shoes with long toes, traced the bells to a type of leather shoe called the Poulaine. It had long thin toe caps and was worn in Poland (then Bohemia). These shoes were very popular during the reign of Richard II (1377-1399) and were probably introduced into England as a result of his marriage to Anne of Bohemia. To draw attention to the pointed shoes: "They were often decorated with a copper bell or a tiny ball that was quite charming and useful during the festive events in the court."

This website dated the fashion from 1360 to 1480. Ruth Hibbard wrote a blog (9/7/2015) for an exhibition of shoes at London's Victoria and Albert Museum in which she also mentioned when the fashion came to an end: "As ever fashions change and at the end of the 15th century it swung full circle and short, square toes (cow's hoof shaped) were now the in thing."

A recent study of 177 medieval adult skeletons in cemeteries in Cambridge, England, showed that this change in fashion could have been influenced by bunions! The research published in the *International Journal of Paleopathology* (11/6/2021) showed that the introduction of poulaines coincided with an epidemic of 'hallux valgus' – a deformation where the big toe bends towards the second toe. This affected balance and mobility and could give rise to bunions!

Dr David Daube, the eminent professor of Law who contributed to the *Oxford Magazine* in 1956, referred to a version of the rhyme written (according to the Opies) around 1790 in which the lady had:

A ring on her finger, a bonnet of straw
The strangest of woman that ever you saw.

He thought the black horse she was riding was a gibbet. This was a "jolly rhyme" about an unpopular hag. "She would be mounted astride on a pole borne by two men and carried through the streets, accompanied by jeering crowds."

Dr Cobham Brewer, the editor of *Brewer's Dictionary of Phrase and Fable*, wrote to the *Sunday Times* (28/6/1893) with a new explanation of the rhyme which he was about to publish in the next edition of the dictionary. "In 1601 the Catholics: ... organised a street procession to the High Cross, Banbury, where a play was about to be performed. The play had scarcely begun when a collision took place with the Puritans and the Catholics had the worst of the fray. The rhyme says let us go to Banbury Cross to see the fun. There will be a fine *lady* on horseback (a terrible scandal indeed to the Puritans). She will have '*rings* on her fingers' (though such ornaments were tabooed by the Puritans) and '*bells* on her toes' to make music, though secular music was wholly forbidden. So despite the law 'she shall have music wherever she goes'."

Using the vital fashion-of-the-time clue it's not difficult to whittle down most of our seven suspects for the fine lady. Out goes Rhiannon – because she dated back long before the slim shoe fashion. Out too goes Lady Godiva – she also lived long before the fashion and she probably wore nothing - not even shoes! Her ride must have been in the 11th century because her husband, Leofric, the Earl of Mercia, died in 1057 and that was in fact before the Coventry cross was built.

Would Queen Elizabeth I have worn shoes that were out of fashion? Probably not. And certainly not if they gave her bunions! Would she have disguised the fact that she looked old? Almost certainly yes. The claim that she was the rider would be much more substantial if it could be shown that she ever rode in triumph through the streets of Banbury.

Katherine Elwes Thomas thought Elizabeth I did go to Banbury on a morale-boosting visit in 1558. This is unlikely since her sister, Queen Mary, died on November 17th of that year and didn't actually reach her grave until after nearly a month of mourning. A lavish funeral was held to consign her to posterity on December 14th. Would there have been time in the remaining two weeks and a bit of that year for a jaunt to Banbury? The new queen would have had Christmas on her mind and her immensely splendid coronation on January 15th high on her to-prepare-for list. Also Queen Elizabeth came to the throne aged 25 – so in no way an 'old woman'.

The *Victorian County History* (1872) in a long section on Banbury mentioned a "proposed itinerary" for a visit by Queen Elizabeth in 1575, when she would have been 41 or 42. But it probably didn't take place as the trip wasn't included in its listing of 20 visits by English monarchs between 1218 and 1647. John Nichols, the author and printer, published in 1788 a detailed account of Queen Elizabeth I's

Progresses and Public Processions. He mentioned over 250 places which she visited. Banbury did not feature among them.

Celia Fiennes, the traveller, writer and explorer on horseback, sounds like a likely candidate for the fine lady but I cannot imagine her wearing bells on her shoes in place of stout no-nonsense riding boots! And she was operating a little bit too late to qualify as the fine lady. She was born in 1662 – more than 60 years after the crosses were destroyed. The Opies were able to contact Geoffrey Rupert Cecil Twistleton-Wykeham-Fiennes, the 19th Baron Saye and Sele, who suspected his father (the 18th Baron of the same name without the 'Rupert') had made the Fiennes Lady up as a joke as he was "a noted wit".

The Lady Katherine Banbury story falls at the first fence. The first Earl of Banbury was William Knollys (a Puritan who might have been the model for Shakespeare's Malvolio in *Twelfth Night*). He was ennobled in 1626, a quarter of a century after the crosses had been destroyed. He didn't have a child who became Lord Jonathan Banbury. And none of his sons married a lady called Katherine as suggested by his distant cousin in New Zealand.

Daube's theory – the unpopular hag on a black horse - is plausible but I have found that his other explanations of nursery rhymes were tongue-in-cheek. The Brewer theory about a clash between Catholics and Puritans is also reasonable if it ever actually occurred. He provided no evidence of this.

I prefer the simplest solution – the May Queen. She is timeless and would have worn rings on her fingers, bells on her shoes, and have had music wherever she went. William Potts wrote in his book about the rhyme: "In the picture of a May Day Riding Party of about the year 1460, preserved in the Musée Condé at [the Château de] Chantilly is represented a gay cavalcade, preceded by trumpeters. The central figure is that of a finely clothed lady riding a white horse….This picture irresistibly suggests the fine lady on the white horse at Banbury Cross. In such a May Riding we see the medieval function on which the rhyme is based, the procession bringing in the may to the town of Banbury with its central figure the May Queen….."

On a rainy Wednesday 27th April 2005 Princess Anne, herself an international prize-winning show jumper, travelled to Banbury unfurled her black umbrella and solemnly unveiled a 13-foot-high bronze statue of a horse with a fine lady on top. To put it more accurately - according to the BBC's local features page on Oxford (updated 24/9/2017) - the actual unveiling was carried out at the princess's command by two members of the Army Cadet Force. The statue, which cost around £180,000, was sculpted by a team from a firm called Artcycle Ltd.

The sculptors had depicted the lady as Queen Guinevere. And this may have been inspired by William Pott's reference to Arthur's queen laying down the rules for riding on May Day in Sir Thomas Malory's *Morte D'Arthur* when she says: "I shall bring with me ten ladies and every knight shall have a lady behind him." This, if you remember, was Potts's definition of riding 'a-cock horse'.

In her unveiling speech, the Princess was reported in the next day's *Oxford Mail* as saying: "Banbury holds a special place in history because it's so well-known through its nursery rhyme and it's extraordinary that for all the time the Cross has been here, there has been no lady on a white horse."

The reason why Banbury took so long to decide the identity of the fine lady is probably because there were so many versions of the rhyme. There is no evidence that the fine lady version of the rhyme appeared before 1797 when it was recollected by Noel Turner in *Infant Institutes*. That was more than 70 years after the first reference to it that we have and more than 50 years after the first time the object of the cock horse rider's quest was first disclosed.

Henry Carey in his satirical poem: *Namby Pamby* (1725), poking fun at a Whiggish poet, wrote: *Now a cock-horse does he ride.* Sadly he didn't say whom the rider was going to see but at least we know the rider was male!

The oldest surviving version of the rhyme was possibly in the very first collection of nursery rhymes *Tom Thumb's Pretty Song Book Volume I* published in 1744. This volume was lost but much of it was reprinted word for word by Isaiah Thomas in his 1788 *Tommy Thumb's Song Book* now in the library of the American Antiquarian Society in Worcester, Massachusetts.

This is the rhyme that most probably was mocked by Henry Carey. It went as follows:

Ride a cock-horse
To Banbury Cross.

To see what Tommy can buy,
A Penny white loaf,
A Penny white cake,
And a Hugey Penny pye.

In the picture that goes with the rhyme in the reprint the rider is a splendid gentleman in fine clothes and a cocked hat riding to see a mystery man or perhaps Tommy Thumb himself – buying a loaf of bread. The old woman or fine lady is not mentioned at all.

Another version in Volume 2 of *Tommy Thumb's Song* Book had the same words as the Worcester version but a different picture of the cock horse rider. It showed a young plump boy in what looks like a dress – who might have been a young Prince George, later George III, according to Andrea Immel and Brian Alderson (2013 *Cotsen Occasional Press*).

So it looks as if the statue that Princess Anne's assistants unveiled should have been a quarter of a mile away from where the present cross stands. It should probably have shown a May Day Queen rather than Queen Guinevere. And the boy who rode 'a-cock horse' to see it could have been her great, great, great, great, great, great, grandfather – long before he lost the Colonies and went mad!

CHAPTER TWELVE

SING A SONG OF SIXPENCE

A dainty royal happy birthday dish

Sing a song of sixpence,
A pocket full of rye;
Four and twenty blackbirds,
Baked in a pie.

And when the pie was opened
The birds began to sing;
Was not that a dainty dish,
To set before the king?

The king was in his counting-house,
Counting out his money;
The queen was in the parlour,
Eating bread and honey.

The maid was in the garden,
Hanging out the clothes,
There came a little blackbird,
And snapped off her nose.

Sing a Song of Sixpence seems nonsensical. How could 24 blackbirds be in any fit state to sing after being baked in a pie? But this can be explained.

For my 76th birthday my granddaughter Cyra, knowing my interest in the Tudors and ignoring my lack of cooking ability, gave me a book called *The Tudor Kitchen*. Written five years earlier in 2015 by Terry Breverton, a prolific Welsh writer, it is full of old recipes.

When I came to research the origins of *Sing a Song of Sixpence* it was one of the first books I consulted. Part 2 of the book (Chapter 12) was headed: 'Dishes You May Not Wish to Cook (or Eat) (or See).' First on the list was 'LIVE BLACKBIRD, RABBIT, FROG, DOG OR DWARF PIE'!

Mr Breverton explained that Tudor cooks baked the crust of a pie before they put in the contents. The crust would rise from the bottom forming a pot shape on to which a baked pastry lid could be placed. "Thus the birds were not," he wrote, "actually cooked in the pie." To amuse the guests, he said, anything could be put inside. Not only were birds put in pies, but rabbits, frogs, dogs and little folk who would pop out and recite poetry. "At one time a whole little musical group emerged to the delight of the diners."

Both Mr Breverton and James Orchard Halliwell in his 1844 collection of nursery rhymes referred readers to a recipe in an Italian cookbook published in English in 1598 called *Epulario or The Italian Banquet*. Written by an Italian chef, Giovanni de Rosselli, in 1516, this book showed how to make pies in pastry coffins that birds may be 'aliue in them, and flie out when it is cut vp'. And fly out they did in what Diana Ferguson wittily captioned "SIXTEENTH-CENTURY BAKE-OFF" in her book *Ring-a-ring O'Roses* (2018).

Katherine Elwes Thomas (*The Real Personages of Mother Goose* 1930) identified the king in the counting-house as Henry VIII gloating over his dissolution of the monasteries. She wrote: "Sing a Song of Sixpence is really Henry's gleeful humming over the confiscated revenues; the 'pocket full of rye', the rich grainfields thus ripening for the royal coffers."

According to her the queen was Catherine of Aragon (wife number one) eating bread and honey - a metaphor for "Spain's cloying assurances that Henry's divorce would not be allowed". The maid was Anne Boleyn (wife number two), in the garden of Whitehall Palace, and the "snipping off of her nose" was accomplished by a "high clerical blackbird" acting on secret commands by Henry himself to break off her engagement to her former boyfriend Lord Henry Percy.

Lady Maxse in *The National Review* (September 1941) identified the blackbird who 'pecked off her nose' as either Cardinal Wolsey, Thomas Cromwell or Archbishop Cramner. Although she added: "I confess I have never understood this *dénouement*." There was one Tudor king who was famous for counting his money: the reputedly miserly Henry VII who bequeathed a fortune for his son Henry VIII to squander. In 2015 the historical fiction writer Judith Arnopp wrote an enjoyable novel called *A Song of Sixpence* which contrasted the lives of one sister and her younger brother: Elizabeth of York who married Henry VII and Richard of York, one of the little princes who 'escaped' from the Tower and masqueraded under the name of Perkin Warbeck.

Arnopp remembered that she was taught as a child that Henry VII and his wife Elizabeth were the king and queen in the song of sixpence. Elizabeth of York, she wrote, took no part in governing the country and her role was a domestic one. Eating bread and honey in the parlour was in keeping with this. At one point halfway through the book Elizabeth listens to a song about a cuckoo and remembers the happier days in her childhood when "I sang to my father for sixpence".

Linda Alchin in *The Secret History of Nursery Rhymes* (2013) noted that the counting house and eating bread and honey were the common man's perception of what a king and queen would spend their time doing. Sandy Leong in *Warts & All* (2018) believed that the rhyme was a populist complaint against the idle rich who had more money than sense. She recounted how live songbirds were folded into the guests' napkins at the Pitti Palace in Florence when Henri IV of France married Marie de Medici in 1600.

According to an article by Susan Moore in *Apollo Magazine* (9/5/2015) no expense was spared in this well-documented marriage. The most distinguished artists of the Medici court vied with each other to produce the most spectacular offerings. On Marie's table a lion, formed out of folded linen, "suddenly rose up on its hind legs and myriad lilies blossomed from its chest". But wouldn't a rhyme which originated from a French Court celebration have started: "Sing a song of *six sous*" rather than sixpence?

The Baring-Goulds in *The Annotated Mother Goose* (1962) mentioned another theory that as the Tudor alphabet had 24 letters (i doubled with j and u with v) the 24 blackbirds were letters set in pica (pie) type and the rhyme celebrated the first printing of the English Bible in 1535.

Jean Harrowven in her book *Origins of Rhymes, Songs and Sayings* (1977) had come across an interesting interpretation of the rhyme which she heard from an old Welsh lady: "It symbolized the passing of night and day: the twenty-four blackbirds represented the number of hours in a full day, the king was the sun and the queen was the moon, when the pie crust was cut it was the sign of a dawning of another day, freeing the birds (hours) to run their course; the coins that the king counted represented the sunbeams, and the bread and honey that the queen ate were the moonbeams; the washing on the line symbolized the clouds in the sky."

The Opies dismissed such allegorical theories. They were "less entertaining" and "too much ink has been expended on them". They referred readers to a witty unattributed story in *The Dictionary of National Biography* that the rhyme could have been poking fun at Henry James Pye who was appointed Poet Laureate in 1790. He wrote one of his customary nauseatingly awful odes in honour of King George III's 52nd birthday that year which was full of allusions to 'vocal groves and feathered choirs'. George Steevens, the 18th century Shakespearean scholar, immediately put out this witty pun on Pye's name: "And when the pie was opened the birds began to sing."

This story was still going the rounds in April 1829 as it was mentioned in a letter written by the essayist Charles Lamb, co-author of *Tales from Shakespeare*. The Oxfordshire town of Faringdon has recently established Blackbird Day in May to celebrate its link to Henry James Pye, who was born and lived there. Its organisers still bake 'blackbird pies' in his honour. The idea of baking special pies and selling them in the May market was the brainwave of Bethia Thomas, Leader of the White Horse Vale City Council. She started this practice about 10 years ago when she was the town's marketing co-ordinator.

Pye's eulogy in 1790 and Steevens' comment about it could not have been the origin of the rhyme as the Opies themselves pointed out. This was because the rhyme featured in James Orchard Halliwell's 1744 collection when George Steevens would have been only eight and James Pye had yet to be born! The rhyme appeared in two early collections of nursery rhymes: on page 8 of *Tommy Thumb's Pretty Song Book* (Volume II) and on page 36 of *Nancy Cocks's Song Book*. In both versions the song wasn't about blackbirds at all!

Sing a Song of Sixpence,
A bag full of Rye,

Four and twenty
Naughty boys,
Bak'd in a Pye.

So who were the naughty boys? This has led to speculation about pirates who could easily have baked these victims. The 'Pirates of the Caribbean' theory was put forward by David Mikkelson on 25th April 1999. He and his wife Barbara run *Snopes.Com*, otherwise known as the 'definitive Internet reference source for researching urban legends, folklore, myths, rumors and misinformation!' Their ingenious theory was that the king was a notorious pirate operating off the West Indies called Captain Blackbeard who died in 1718 before he was 40. The song was a clever ditty used in taverns to recruit pirates. They would be paid sixpence a day along with a bottle of whisky (rye). The four and twenty blackbirds (or naughty boys) were pirates hiding in a pie ready to spring out.

Misinformation! I should have known that pirates in those days dealt mainly in rum and that rye whisky only originated in Pittsburgh in the late 18th century.

Interviewed in the *New York Times* in July 2010 David Mikkelson was asked if he indulged in rumours. He replied: "Yes. Just to see if people would spread them. So, we made up, from whole cloth, this legend about the nursery rhyme, 'Sing a song of sixpence'. About how it was a secret code that pirates used to recruit members for their crew in taverns. I have seen this quoted in books. I've seen this presented as fact on television shows. Even on urban legend-related television shows (they) have claimed this as true. But it just shows that this is now proffered as the real explanation behind that nursery rhyme."

It's likely that the rhyme predated Captain Blackbeard by at least a century. James Orchard Halliwell pointed out in his rhyme collections that it was almost certainly referred to in John Fletcher's *Bonduca* – his tragicomedy about Queen Boudica (or Boadicea) and her general Caratach (Caractacus). Almost at the end of the play (Act V scene 2) when one of Boudica's daughters has committed suicide, her lover Petillius , a general, enters the stage very depressed. To cheer him up, a fellow officer Junius suggests: 'Let me sing then.' To which Petillius replies: "Whoa, here's a stir now: *sing a song o' six pence.*"

This play was first performed by the King's Men around 1613 and published in the first Beaumont and Fletcher folio in 1647. Another possible reference to the song (also mentioned by Halliwell in his 1843 edition) appears in Shakespeare's *Twelfth Night* (1601-02). In Act II Scene 3 Sir Toby Belch says to the fool: "Come on; there is sixpence for you; let's have a song."

If the rhyme was already circulating at the end of the Tudor period, then which bit of it was circulating? It could have been the one verse in *Tommy Thumb's Pretty Song Book* (Volume II) mentioned above with the naughty boys being baked. Or it could have been the version of the rhyme in the first volume of *Tommy Thumb's Song Book* also published in 1744. This book has been lost, but many believe a version of it was reprinted by Isaiah Thomas, the American antiquarian, in 1788. This version of the rhyme had the first two verses as quoted at the top of this chapter with the four and twenty blackbirds rather than the naughty boys.

The earliest surviving mention of the king counting his money and the queen eating bread and honey came in 1784 when Joseph Ritson included them in *Gammer Gurton's Garland* . My hunch is that the verses about the counting house, the queen, the parlour and the maid were added later.

If the Isaiah Thomas version was the original version of the rhyme we can exclude the subsequent verses in trying to find the identity of the king. He might not have had a queen. But those first two verses in themselves contain some important clues:

1. It's a song of sixpence not for sixpence. So I have translated this as a song about a sixpence rather than a song for which the payment was 6d.

2. The first sixpence was minted in 1551.

3. It's a song in which a dainty dish was set before a certain king possibly to celebrate an event.

If the rhyme is a Tudor one, there are only three Tudor kings to choose from: Henry VII, Henry VIII and Edward VI. Did any of them have a special connection with the sixpence?

Henry VIII in his later years needed more money even though he had dissolved the monasteries. He resorted to robbing the currency, debasing the silver in the coins by two thirds and replacing it with copper. The debasement of the coinage

(1544-1547) "was the greatest act of monetary treason in history," wrote Catherine Downey, a university undergraduate, in the *Student Economic Review* (1997). It was widely unpopular. And Henry earned the nickname 'Old Coppernose' according to Owen James in *Quantative easing the medieval way* published by the Royal Mint in 2012. Henry's face – particularly his nose apparently - on the coin (known as a Testoon or Teston) when rubbed became red as the silver coating wore off. This caused a famous epigram from John Heywood, the Tudor poet and playwright:

These Testons look redde: how like you the same?
T'is a token of grace: they blush for shame.

But relief was at hand. The ministers who ruled when Henry's son came to the throne in 1547 set about reforming the currency and in October 1551 the debasement policy was officially revoked. The much-hated testoon was replaced by a popular good quality fully silver coin – the King Edward VI sixpence. *Royalmint.com* commented: "The coin quickly became a symbol of prosperity and good fortune."

Its birth was referred to in King Edward's diary the day after his 14th birthday. It followed a major event, the ennobling of the new Duke of Suffolk. This precocious, highly intelligent, young sovereign recorded events which he thought were important as they happened almost daily throughout the last three years of his reign. His 'chronicle' is now in the British Library and using a microfiche version of it I was able to enlarge his spidery and often faded writing. There are several entries in it on the decline of the teston from 12d to 6d as he took a keen interest in his coinage. On the 13th October 1551 he wrote as follows: "Proclamation signed touching the calling in of testornes and grotes (groats), that they that list might cu (?come) to the minte and have fine silver of twelve pence for tow (two) testornes."

Sadly it was his second last birthday as he died on July 6th 1553. He did not record how he celebrated it. It would have been the perfect occasion for a new song to be sung - 'of sixpence' not 'for 6d' - and a dainty pie to be baked in his and the new coin's honour.

CHAPTER THIRTEEN

THREE BLIND MICE

Silly fools or brave martyrs?

Three blind mice, see how they run!
They all ran after the farmer's wife,
Who cut off their tails with a carving knife,
Did you ever see such a thing in your life.
As three blind mice?

Mary I ('Bloody Mary') has a lot to answer for without adding another crime to her infamy! She had about 300 Protestant martyrs executed for heresy and then lost the French port of Calais – England's last foothold in France. Now in *Three Blind Mice* she's called a farmer's wife and accused of callous cruelty to three tiny animals with a carving knife!

But this accusation is unfair. There's hardly a shred of evidence to link her to the crime and rhyme. The slander was probably first spread by Katherine Elwes Thomas, who, as I have shown elsewhere in this book, wasn't always historically accurate. She decreed that the mice were poor blind Protestant rodents: Archbishop Thomas Cranmer and the two bishops Nicholas Ridley and Hugh Latimer. They were burnt at the stake in the mid-16th century on the orders of the Catholic queen.

The episcopal trio bravely met their death in Broad Street, Oxford, at a site opposite Balliol College which is now marked by a sunken iron cross in the road. They weren't despatched at the same time which immediately made me suspicious of their connection with the rhyme. Cranmer was taken to the tower of the Bocardo Prison in the Cornmarket where he was forced to watch the burning of Ridley and Latimer on the 16th October 1555. It was hoped he would recant so his execution was delayed until 21st March 1556. He recanted on several occasions but at the last moment he memorably stretched out the hand which signed the recantation into the fire so it would burn first.

'They all ran after the farmer's wife': Elwes Thomas had read the 16th century religious writer and historian Sir Richard Baker's *Chronicles of the Kings of England* (1665) in the Bodleian Library and concluded from them that the abbey lands which Queen Mary restored to the Catholic church were full of 'prosperous farms'. She wrote: "In thus redistributing the priory and abbey lands among her cardinals and priests, Mary is the typical 'farmer's wife' with the then universally contemptuous epithet of 'mice' applied to the clergy."

Nursery rhyme detectives Albert Jack, Linda Alchin, and Sandy Leong, all following the Elwes Thomasian theory, mentioned as a vital clue that Mary's unpopular husband got his nickname in the rhyme because he owned vast estates in Spain and elsewhere. But to call Philip II (Mary's husband and Emperor of Spain) 'a farmer' was vastly belittling his imperial status as the Spanish empire was one of the largest in history! Thomas herself, not one to underplay gossip, added a bit of ribaldry suggesting that Mary (the farmer's wife) was secretly wed to her Lord Chancellor, Stephen Gardiner.

The three clerics are described in the rhyme as running after Mary. What does this mean? Albert Jack explained: "Openly Catholic, Mary was seen as a real danger to newly Protestant England, and the policies set in motion by these three were openly unfriendly: in effect, They all ran after the farmer's wife."

Certainly, in that sense, they had 'run after' her for many years. On May 23rd 1533 when Mary was only 17, Thomas Cranmer, Archbishop of Canterbury, declared the marriage of Mary's parents Henry VIII and Catherine of Aragon null and void before going on to proclaim the union with Anne Boleyn legal five days later, thus making Mary illegitimate.

Three days after her brother Edward VI, the boy king, was proclaimed dead on July 6th 1553, Ridley, then Bishop of London, preached a sermon at St Paul's Cross, London, affirming that the Princess Elizabeth was also a bastard. All three bishops at that time supported the succession of the Protestant Lady Jane Grey as queen in Mary's place.

'Who cut off their tails with a carving knife'. How could this fate have happened to three human bishops? Elwes Thomas wrote rather lamely: "The cutting off of their tails was figuratively accomplished in the burning at the stake."

'Did you ever see such a thing in your life?' This could be descriptive of the reaction to the horror with which the executions of these three holy men (later known as the Oxford martyrs) were greeted by the common people. John Foxe in his *Book of Martyrs* (1563) reporting on the deaths of Latimer and Ridley wrote: "Every eye shed tears at the afflicting sight of these sufferers who were among the most distinguished persons of their time in dignity, piety and public estimation."

'As three blind mice!' This is where the Bloody Marian explanation falls apart. None of them were blind. Unless you take a rather unconvincing and uncharacteristic Catholic slant to the rhyme which says: 'they were blind to the truth'. They could of course have been blindfolded. This happened at beheadings but not at burnings as far as one can judge from pictures. In Foxe's records of these three martyrs' deaths there is no record of blindfolds.

Among Foxe's 284 listed victims of the Marian persecutions were four who were described as actually blind. This led Chris Roberts in *Heavy Words Lightly Thrown* (2004) to speculate for a moment that the rhyme might have referred to the burnings of Joan Waste and John Aprice. Joan, despite her blindness, was a rope-maker from Derby. She could also knit. She bought an English translation of the *New Testament* and paid a penny a time for her friends to read it to her. She also publicly denied the doctrine of transubstantiation. She met her fate in Derby on August 1st 1556. John Aprice (or Apprice) was burnt at Stratford, London, for rejecting the teachings of the church on 15th May 1556. Another blind person, Thomas Drowry, a lad of 16, was also burnt around that time in Gloucester. Elizabeth, a blind maid, possibly surnamed Lewis, was put to death in Maidstone the next year. But none of their deaths caused as much of a stir as the three bishops.

The Baring-Goulds writing in 1962 noted that: "Some attempts, few of them convincing, have been made to read significance into *Three Blind Mice*. Thus 'the farmer's wife' becomes Queen Mary I of England, so called because she was a woman of large landed properties."

There was no hint of the Marian Martyrs in the rhyme about three blind mice when it first surfaced in a collection of 33 musical melodies collected by Thomas Ravenscroft. *Deuteromelia*, published in 1609 – 50 years or so after Queen Mary's death – was his second great musical collection. Ravenscroft was a pioneer collector of songs and rhymes and author of two learned works on the theory of music.

Instead of a farmer's wife, *Deuteromelia's* most famous rhyme featured a 14th century much-venerated anchoress (hermit) called Dame Julian (or Iulian) of Norwich.

There was also a miller and his merry wife who scraped a plate of tripe and licked the knife clean afterwards. The words in his collection went as follows:

> *Three Blinde Mice, three Blinde Mice,*
> *Dame Iulian, Dame Iulian,*
> *The Miller and his merry olde Wife,*
> *she scrapte her tripe; licke thou the knife.*
> *Three Blinde Mice, three Blinde Mice.*

Robin P. Nettelhorst, an American pastor from Quartz Hill, California, and author of several religious books, has three daughters. One day when he was sitting with his middle daughter in a paediatrician's waiting-room she noticed a painting of the nursery rhyme on the wall. She wondered who had written it, what it might be about and when it might have been composed.

In an extract headlined 'Catching Fog' on the internet (4/5/2013) he referred to the idea that the rhyme was about the martyrs and wondered why if this were true it had taken more than 50 years for the rhyme to emerge. He blogged: "Unfortunately for the theory, the three bishops, Ridley, Latimer and Cranmer were not, in fact, blinded. Instead they were burned at the stake. Beyond that, there's the simple fact that the lyrics are dated a few years *after* Mary had died, so it's hard to see why a song would have been made up about her at such a late date. Others have suggested that the song somehow references the beliefs of Julian of Norwich, since she is mentioned in the original lyrics."

Dame Julian of Norwich was one of the greatest mystics of her age. She fell seriously ill on the 8th May 1373 when she was 30. A priest was holding a crucifix in front of her and administering the last rites when she began to lose her sight and felt physically numb but gazing on the crucifix she saw the figure of Jesus beginning to bleed. She then had 16 visions over the next day or so. She had completely recovered by May 13th. These visions then inspired her book: *Revelations of Divine Love* in which her most famous saying was: "Alle shalle be wele, and alle manner of thing shall be wele."

Although none of the visions appear to be about mice, blind or otherwise, Dame

Julian had a cat according to Sharon Bennett Connolly, tour guide and author. Writing on the internet (5/4/2020) under the headline: *Dame Julian of Norwich: All shall be well* Connolly wrote: "She was also allowed to keep a cat, to control the mice and rats; many images of Julian show her dressed in the habit of a nun, with a cat sat at her feet as she studies her books."

But did this cat exist? In 1989 Professor Mary E Little, of Central Florida University, wrote a children's book entitled: *Julian's Cat: The Imaginary History of a Cat of Destiny*. But in 2008 in a series of essays about Dame Julian, Dr Sarah Salih, Co-director of the Centre for Late Antique and Medieval Studies at King's College, London University, described the cat as "an invention" and an attempt to modernise Dame Julian and make her cosier than the "enclosed career virgin and learned theologian she was".

The farmer's wife version of the rhyme did not materialise publicly for another 133 years after Ravenscroft's *Deuteromelia*. James Orchard Halliwell included the first three lines only (ending with carving-knife) in his 1842 collection of nursery rhymes. The Opies said that as "far as has been ascertained" this was the first time the new words to the rhyme appeared in children's literature.

At that time Britain was ruled by George III. He was nick-named 'Farmer George', a witty pun because of his interest in agriculture. The 'farmer's wife' could have been his wife, Queen Charlotte of Mecklenburg-Strelitz . But as Norman Iles pointed out in *Who Really Killed Cock Robin* (1986) the original lines in *Deuteromilia* predated all the Georgian kings of Britain by more than 100 years. In fact this future queen (born in 1844) would have been minus two-years-old when the farmer's wife version of the rhyme was thought to have first appeared!

It's unlikely that someone would at the start of Queen Victoria's reign be writing a skit on the Marian persecutions when the 'bloody' queen had been in her grave for nearly 300 years. The Dame Julian version of the rhyme does not seem to make much sense and maybe it was never intended that it should. The Opies found a suggestion in a famous 19th century diary that the mice in the rhyme were more like 'mickey mice' in other words 'worthless'.

When the Scottish diarist James Boswell came to London in 1762, aged 21, he was befriended by a fair-weather friend called Alexander Montgomerie. He was the 10th Earl of Eglinton. He introduced the young Boswell to various clubs including the Noblemen and Gentlemen's Catch Club. This had been founded in 1761 to encourage the composition and performance of ancient songs and rhymes known as 'glees, catches and canons'. But the noble lord also had over a long period promised to help Boswell get a commission in the army. On the 15th March 1763 he even undertook to ask the then Prime Minister, Lord Bute, for a commission in The Guards for him and then asked Boswell if he believed him.

Boswell recorded his reply in his *London Journal* : "No my Lord. Be not afraid that I always believe your Lordship in the past tense but never in the future. When you say I have done so & so, I make no doubt of it. But when you say I will do so & so, Your Lordship must excuse me. I believe you intend to do what you say; But perhaps the Song of the '*Three blind mice*' comes across you & prevents you from thinking of it."

A further clue that the rhyme was considered nonsense was the description of the Dame Julian rhyme by Thomas Oliphant, a Scottish musician, artist, and author, who was president of the Madrigal Society in 1871 for two years before his death. He included the Dame Julian version of *Three Blind Mice* in his 1837 collection of madrigals, ballets and roundelays. He commented in 1843: "This absurd old round is frequently brought to mind in the present day, from the circumstance of there being an instrumental Quartet by Weiss, through which runs a musical phrase accidentally the same as the notes applied to the words *Three Blind Mice*."

Three Blind Mice today is still a popular 'round' where a minimum of three voices sing the song. Each singer starts at a different line in the song. In his third collection of nursery rhymes in 1844 Halliwell referenced *Deuteromelia* as the original source of the song and added a fourth and all-revealing line:

> *Did you ever see such fools in your life?*

It wasn't clever of the mice to chase the farmer's wife. They were looking for trouble. Mice do not usually run after those trying to catch them except perhaps in *Tom and Jerry* cartoons. These mice were not brave martyrs but silly foolish creatures. Bloody Mary had nothing to do with them.

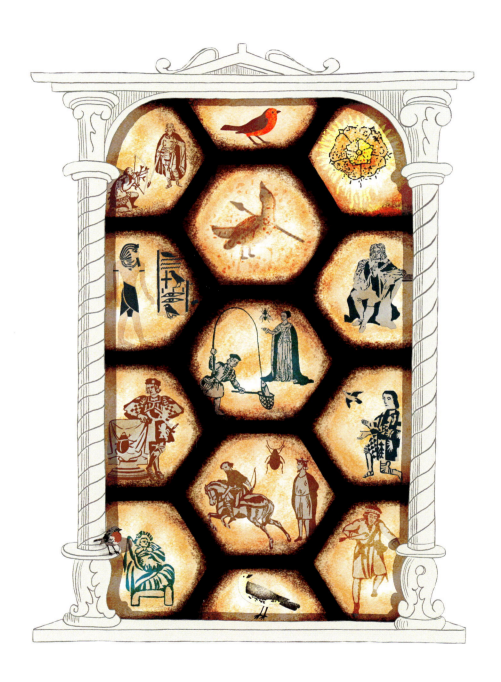

CHAPTER FOURTEEN
WHO KILLED COCK ROBIN?
Nursery Rhymes' Who Dunnit

Who killed Cock Robin?
I, said the Sparrow,
With my bow and arrow,
I killed Cock Robin.

Who saw him die?
I, said the Fly,
With my little eye,
I saw him die.

Who caught his blood?
I said the Fish,
With my little dish,
I caught his blood.

Who'll make the shroud?
I, said the Beetle,
With my thread and needle,
I'll make the shroud.

I end my trail of favourite nursery rhymes with a mystery death. Who killed Cock Robin? Who was the sparrow? Who were the witnesses to the killing – the fly who saw him die, the fish who somehow held up a dish to catch his blood – and who was the beetle who made his shroud? And above all who was poor Cock Robin?

It's one of our oldest nursery rhymes. *Who did kill Cock Robin* was in *Tommy Thumb's Pretty Song Book* (Volume 2) compiled by Mary Cooper in 1744. It had only the four verses printed above. The same lines were in the version that Isaiah Thomas published in Worcester, Massachusetts in 1788 which may have been a reprint of Cooper's original volume 1. It later became a much longer poem when several more birds were added. They officiated at the funeral and mourned the much-loved corpse.

Coincidentally – or maybe this was the origin of the rhyme - there was in fact a political downfall two years before the rhyme first surfaced in the *Song Books*. It was the fall of the 'Robinocracy' as it was dubbed by lampoonists at the time. This was the end of Robert Walpole's government in 1742. He was called Britain's first Prime Minister because he was the first head of government to combine two great offices of State – Leader of the Commons and Chancellor of the Exchequer. He was much loved in his time but brought down after a spell of unpopularity by his fellow Whigs and then widely mourned.

But there is evidence that the rhyme is much older than the 18th century. The Opies pointed out: "Indications, internal and external, suggest that the rhyme has some antiquity". In the fifth verse 'Owl' rhymes with 'shovel'. In the medieval period 'shovell' was pronounced 'shoul' or 'shouall' and would have rhymed with owl.

There are stained glass windows dating from the late medieval end of the 15th century in an old priest's house, the Old Buckland Rectory in Gloucestershire, built around 1480 according to *British Listed Buildings*. It's one of the oldest surviving former rectory buildings in the country.

An article in the *British Archaeological Association Journal* in July 1944 featured the pictures of birds in medieval stained-glass windows. It was written by the Reverend Christopher Woodforde, chaplain at New College, Oxford, and Dean of Wells. He was an authority on English stained and painted glass, including those with birds depicted on them.

He wrote: "It is possible that a quarry [small pane of glass] in Buckland rectory illustrates a nursery rhyme. It shows a bird pierced through the breast by an arrow. This by itself would not be enough to point to the rhyme, for birds were shot at with bows and arrows as well as snared. But the glass picture has given the bird the markings of a robin. The rhyme *Who killed cock robin?* has not, however, been traced back to a date earlier than the eighteenth century."

With the help of Patrick McCanlis, the church warden at the ancient St Michael's Church nearby, I arranged to see the owners of the Old Rectory, Buckland, in February 2023. They have restored the house since they moved into it about 30 years ago. They told me that when they bought it they had no idea that it could possibly be connected to a nursery rhyme but a few years ago they had a visit from a Japanese student who was writing a thesis on the origin of nursery rhymes.

The hall of the Old Rectory was impressively hammer-beamed with ends descending into wooden carved angels. But far above my head the window markings at the top of this pair of windows seemed very faintly etched in a sepia colour, almost vanishing into the opaque glass. Chris Deacon-Davis, the rectory's South African gardener, arrived wearing a khaki green T-shirt with the motto: "I'm sexy and I mow it!". But more importantly he was carrying a large metal stepladder.

I climbed up it. The two windows themselves contained eight panes of glass, iron-framed, each transparent with nothing on them. The clues to the rhyme, if they were clues, were interspersed into the smaller arched stone triptychs consisting of four small panes at the very top. In the centre of the one on the right window was the best-preserved coloured pane. It featured a white rose with a beautiful yellow centre surrounded by the rays of a golden shining sun. This was the white rose of York. It depicted the badge of the then Plantagenet king. The other frames in this window top contained faded sepia bird shapes – difficult to distinguish as to their type. But three sunrays at the bottom had been elongated possibly on purpose. Could this be a representation of a meteorological phenomenon known as parhelion? This heralded Edward IV's hard-fought victory at the Battle of Mortimer's Cross in Hertfordshire on 2nd February 1461.

The other window's triptych arched top had birds where the shapes were a little clearer. The one at the centre top had a longish beak like that of a gull. Below, the one on the left had a long neck and the arrow seemed to be whizzing past the top of its left wing. But the one in the middle could well have had the markings of a robin. The arrow shot from above had landed deep into its neck. The bird in the other right-hand frame was unharmed and could possibly have been a sparrow!

What were these birds doing at a time when the house belonged to a man of God - not the most likely person to spend his weekends on a country shoot! What was he thinking when he chose those panes for the window. Was he trying to tell us a story?

There is one king who died unexpectedly in mysterious circumstances aged 40 around the time that the stained-glass window appeared in that timbered hall in Gloucestershire: Edward IV. His badge and sunny emblem are commemorated in the right-hand window. How did he die on 9th April 1483? No one really knows. Until recently many historians believed he died from a mysterious illness – a disease unknown to the doctors who tended him.

His death would have caused a lot of gossipy theories. Although fat through heavy drinking and debauchery, he did not appear to show any symptoms of illness before Easter (April 1st) of that year. Some thought he died from a culmination of loose living, and some from apoplexy caused by the French King's reneging on a possible treaty with England, some from a stroke and some from a chill. Annette Carson, author of a book about his younger brother - *Richard III: The Maligned King* (2008) - believes Edward IV was poisoned with arsenic. News of his death managed to reach York a few days before he died suggesting that the first attempt to kill him went wrong.

Edward's once beautiful queen, Elizabeth Woodville, had been supplanted by many mistresses. She may have been the fly 'that saw him die'. Her family were losing the influence they had had on the king and in the weeks before he died Elizabeth's brother-in-law, Lord Anthony Rivers, had sought copies of letters patent confirming his governorship of the heir to the throne, later the short-lived Edward V. Lord Rivers also appointed another of his nephews to control the Tower of London without the king's consent for which he would have been punished if the king had been living. Could he have been the sparrow?

And the beetle who 'made his shroud'? Could he have been Edward IV's younger brother Richard, who in the end benefited from his death, and became Richard III. And the fish who 'caught his blood' may have been just that - a fish. Many centuries later in 1934 an account of the 'usurpation' of Richard III was found in a French library in Lille. It had been written by an Italian friar, Domenico Mancini, working for a French bishop who reported to the French King Louis XI. Mancini had been in London and based his reports on gossip currently doing the rounds at the time. He reported that Edward IV had "allowed the damp cold to strike his vitals" and died from a chill caught on a fishing trip.

I sent photographs of the stained-glass windows to the British Ornithological Trust for examination by their experts. They said the artistic impressions had slightly stumped them. The one with the arrow through its neck could have been a woodcock (not a robin) and so could the one on the right given its "cryptic patterning and long bill". The glass looked as if it had been made of remnants reused from elsewhere as the glass panes "seem out of context with the trefoil shape of the masonry". The date of the windows suggest that they could have been added later after the dissolution of the monasteries (1536-41).

The expert went on to say: "If it did relate to 'Who Killed Cock Robin' remember that only the robin was a victim, so why three birds? Therefore, even if one bird is thought to have been a robin, this doesn't explain the others. This, along with the date as you have said, further suggests that the window was retrospectively linked to the nursery rhyme. I hope that helps and sorry we can't give a more precise answer on the IDs of the birds."

Jean Harrowven, who wrote a book about the historical origins of nursery rhymes in 1977, had also followed up this theory and come to the same conclusion. She had contacted the Reverend Michael Bland then Rector of Buckland, who was certain the birds in the window were not robins but blackcocks. She said the link between the panes and the rhyme "was rather remote to say the least".

Her candidate for Cock Robin was an earlier medieval king and unlike Edward IV he had really been killed by an arrow. According to Henry of Huntingdon, the 12th century English historian, who wrote *Historia Anglorum* (History of the English) it all began with a fiery sermon by the first abbot of Shrewsbury on the morning of August 1st 1100. Abbot Fulchred of Séez fulminated against the anti-clerical William II, nicknamed Rufus, the son of William the Conqueror who was quarrelling with Anselm, the Archbishop of Canterbury, at the time. He preached: "Behold the bow of divine anger is bent against the wicked and the arrow swift is taken from the quiver."

William of Malmesbury, another 12th century English historian, recorded how that night William Rufus had had a nightmare about a surgeon who was letting out his blood. It took on a terrifying tone according to the modern-day historian Charles Spencer in his book *The White Ship* (2020).

Nevertheless the next day, Thursday August 2nd, the royal party, as Spencer described, set out on a hunting expedition in the New Forest in Hampshire despite further warnings from the Abbot of Gloucester that the monks at his abbey had had troubling dreams last night that the king would soon be punished by God.

In the party was a French knight called Walter Tirel. No one knows what happened exactly as Tirel said he was in another part of the forest at the time. But he is credited with firing the fatal arrow which accidentally or by design struck William Rufus fatally in the chest. Nearby on that day also 'in another part of the forest' was his younger brother Henry, who immediately after the accident hurried off to Winchester and proclaimed himself King Henry I. Could he have been the beetle that made the shroud?

Jean Harrowven wrote: "The song is known to be of great antiquity and there is no justifiable reason to doubt its association with William Rufus ….. Some historians believe that William Rufus was a pagan and that he was killed deliberately, as the sacred king who had to be sacrificed on Lammastide."

Lammastide begins in the Northern Hemisphere on August 1st and William died on August 2nd. Also, William was nick-named Rufus because he had red hair which could provide a link with robin redbreast.

However as with other nursery rhymes the question arises as to why it should take so long for Cock Robin to be associated with William II. There is no other evidence and although William II is a more likely cock robin candidate than Edward IV the more I read about the rhyme the more it seemed to have connotations with a past more ancient and more international than the Norman and Plantagenet kings of England.

The idea of birds flocking to a funeral originates from ancient times. Lina Eckenstein's comparison of rhymes across different countries was inspired, according to *The Oxford Dictionary of National Biography,* by the resemblance of the burial of King Seti I in an ancient Egyptian temple to the death and burial of Cock Robin 3,000 years later.

Seti I's tomb is one of the best-decorated in the Valley of the Kings in the desert near Luxor. Visiting it in October 2022 I stepped into the multi-layered vault of this fearsome Pharoah, who died aged 40 in 1279 BC. Deep down, where his decapitated mummified body once lay, the tops of the walls are adorned by four large portrayals of the winged goddess ISIS and her three sisters. Beneath them is a frieze running across the four walls. At the top it contains flocks of birds in much larger numbers than at any other tomb in the Pyramids. This must have been where Eckenstein gained the idea of the resemblance to the death of Cock Robin.

The birds were not only going to a funeral but helping Seti I pass on to the next world. Our tour guide, Sabry Abdel Azem, who trained in Egyptology, explained: "Birds were a linguistic symbol of the Egyptian hieroglyphic book and some of these birds were sanctified such as the ibis, hoopoe, owl, falcon, and eagle. They were embalmed and often portrayed as gods. They were needed by Seti as protection to accompany him to the after-life as described in the *Emy-Duat,* the book of hours and of what is in the other world. On these four walls we see the second, third and fourth hours of his one-day passage when Seti is passing through the Waters of Osiris."

Eckernstein wrote: "The antiquity of this knell of the robin is apparent when we come to compare it with its foreign parallels which are current in France, Italy and Spain." Each of these is about the funeral of a bird and the chief mourners. The rhyme which she found in Mecklenburg, Germany, is strikingly similar. It begins: 'Wer is dod?' (Who is dead?) and two of its lines in particular are similar to the Cock Robin rhyme:

> *Kukuk is de kulengräver* [The Cuckoo is the grave digger]
> *Adebor is de klokkentreder,* [The Stork is the bellringer]

But this is not the only poem about the death of Cock Robin. *The Courtship, Merry Marriage, and Picnic Dinner of Cock Robin and Jenny Wren* was published as a toy book (an illustrated book for children) by John Harris in 1810. This had an addendum: *The doleful death of the bridegroom* which described a dreadful accident at the wedding attended by the same kind of birds as in the other rhyme:

> *When in came the Cuckoo,*
> *And made a great rout;*
> *He caught hold of Jenny,*
> *And pulled her about.*
> *Cock Robin was angry,*
> *And so was the Sparrow,*
> *Who fetch'd in a hurry*
> *His Bow and his Arrow.*
> *His aim then he took;*
> *But he took it not right:*
> *His skill was not good,*
> *Or he shot in a fright;*
> *For the Cuckoo he miss'd,*
> *But Cock Robin he kill'd! -*
> *And all the Birds mourn'd*
> *That his blood was so spill'd.*

It was all the cuckoo's fault! Lina Eckenstein reminded us that the cuckoo was the bird of the Norse god Thor who was the enemy of matrimonial bliss. Some interpreters have traced the rhyme back to the death of a much-loved god of light called Baldur. Norse gods were not immortal as Chris Roberts reminded us in *Heavy Words Lightly Thrown* (2003). Baldur dreamt that he would die from a grave misfortune. His dream "was taken very seriously. The other gods thought of everything that might possibly cause Baldur harm, from diseases to creatures and weapons. With a list in hand, Baldur's mother, Frigg, set out to exact assurances from these entities that they would not harm Baldur."

However, she had not included mistletoe because she thought it "too small and inconsequential". Maybe she didn't know it was poisonous. During the feast, the gods playfully tested out this promise by throwing sticks and rocks and anything else that came to hand at Baldur. They all bounced off him and it seemed good fun. But then Loki, the god of mischief and adopted son of Odin, found out from Frigg that she had not bothered to include mistletoe. He made a spear out of a mistletoe branch and gave it to his brother Hod, the blind god, and helped him with his aim. It was fatal. Baldur died. His wife overcome with grief died with him. They were both burnt on his ship which was turned into a great funeral pyre.

But there is no link here with the name: Cock Robin. Another god has been linked to the rhyme. Celtic tradition placed Lugh as the sun god with a traditional feast on Lammas Day (August 1st) which was marked in an old calendar by a bow and arrow shape. The astronomer, Martin Griffiths, Director of the Brecon Beacons Observatory, described the night sky and "the lesser-known stories of the stars" on the website *lablit.com* on 13th January 2008: "As Lugh was the primary god representing the red sun, his name in common parlance would have been 'Coch Rhi Ben' anglicised to 'Cock Robin' – a leftover from the belief that souls became birds after death. This idea is still sustained in the old folk song 'Who Killed Cock Robin' in which the sparrow kills him with "my bow and arrow", the sparrow here representing Bran, the tanist incarnation or opposite of Lugh – the god of winter."

I'm not entirely convinced. If Cock Robin and the Sparrow were based on real characters, human or mythological, their identities have been lost in the mist of time - perhaps in one of those ancient legends. As Oliver Tearle, lecturer, author, and nursery rhyme expert, wrote in *Britain by the Book* (2017): "It's nearly always impossible to pin down a nursery rhyme's origins in any definite way."

I'm sad to end this book with an unsolved whodunnit! With some nursery rhymes like *Pop Goes the Weasel*, *Three Blind Mice* and in my last book *Hey Diddle Diddle*, there's fairly compelling evidence that these rhymes, like many other nursery rhymes, are nonsense and were never intended to have any meaning.

In others *The Lion and the Unicorn* and in my last book *The Grand Old Duke of York* there is good evidence that they were based on real historical characters. And in my last book *Mary Mary Quite Contrary* and in this book *Sing a Song of Sixpence* I have come up with new theories, based mainly on linguistics, which have not been put forward before. For the rest I have put forward as many theories I could find and come up with the most likely solution out of the ones that have been put forward.

This happened with *Little Jack Horner* and in the process I hope I have convinced you that the present squire of a Somerset manor is not living in stolen property. It was the widespread rumour that *Ring a Ring o'Roses* must have been about the Great Plague (1665) that first started me on the trail which led to my writing *Cracking Humpty Dumpty* (available on www.humptycracked.com).

I have been concerned to expose spoof theories - many of them tongue in cheek many of them humorous, and all of them fun. Discussion of these will, I hope, inspire even more theories and prolong the enjoyment we can all have from nursery rhymes which must be one of the most enduring and colourful legacies which British jinglers have passed on to the rest of the English-speaking world. But for how much longer? Please read my epilogue.

EPILOGUE

OLD SOLDIERS NEVER DIE?

Mother Goose or nursery rhymes are like old soldiers. There is a traditional army ballad whose final lines begin: *Old Soldiers never die*. And this was the proud boast (you may remember from my introduction) contained in an old copy of *Mother Goose's Melody*: "No, No, my Melodies will never die, while nurses sing, or babies cry."

But the line *Old Soldiers never die….* ends with the words: *they simply fade away*.

In 50 years' time will nursery rhymes, like Aesop's fables, simply fade away and become an academic relic of our distant past? Will Humpty Dumpty become a bit like the hare who lost to the tortoise in a rather quaint race? As long as *The Mousetrap* continues its long 70-plus year run in London so the thespian *cognoscenti* may fondly recall that it owes its origins to a 30-minute radio play by Agatha Christie called *Three Blind Mice* first broadcast in 1947. But who else will care? Will nursery rhymes vanish away like some of the pubs which were once called *The Cat and Fiddle* and *The Duke of York*?

In 2009 the Nation's Favourite Rhyme Survey was undertaken by the Book Trust charity and involved 2,500 parents in Britain. The survey found that more than a third of parents had never sung a nursery rhyme to their children and more than a quarter of them could not remember a single rhyme from their childhood. Many parents preferred modern pop songs to sing with their children as nursery rhymes were seen to be too 'old-fashioned'. *The Daily Telegraph* covered the story (7/10/2009) with the headline: **Traditional nursery rhymes could be heading for extinction.** In 2022, just 13 years later, MAM, the baby products manufacturer, carried out a similar survey among 2000 parents aged 26 to 41. The results were even more dismal for the future of nursery rhymes. Only 53% could recite *Baa Baa Black Sheep*, less than a half knew *Humpty Dumpty* and about the same percentage could recite the first verse of *Twinkle, Twinkle, Little Star*.

The *Daily Mail* ran the headline: **Are millennials putting lullabies to sleep for good?** Both research projects centred on parents. Neither covered how far today's children come into contact with nursery rhymes through their playgroup or school, from the media and on the internet without their parents participating. Even so the passing of nursery rhyme knowledge from parent to child would seem to me to be crucial if nursery rhymes are to continue to exist.

Does it matter if nursery rhymes are themselves being slowly put to sleep? Is there any evidence that repeating such rhymes are good for children's education and early development? Or have they just outlived their 18th century usefulness?

In 2004 Professor Kathy Sylva, Professor of Educational Psychology at Oxford University, led a study of 3,000 children between the ages of three and seven to investigate the effects of pre-school education. She found that the children of parents who reported "teaching songs and nursery rhymes" went on to higher achievement at school and showed better social adjustment.

Professor Roger Beard was a consultant to the 2009 Book Trust survey and was then Head of the School of Early Childhood and Primary Education at the University of London's Institute of Education. He summed up the importance of nursery rhymes in his book *Language Play and Children's Literacy*, which he co-authored in 2021. He wrote: "Many nursery rhymes have an enduring appeal and 'memorability' that appeals to young children across generations. There is also substantial evidence that, as well as helping to form a loving bond between parent/carers and children, the experience of listening to and recalling such rhymes can play a vital role in children's language development."

The journalist Damon Syson wrote in *The Times* two months after the 2009 survey was published: "Numerous studies report a significant relationship between nursery rhyme knowledge at the age of 3 and success in reading and spelling at 5 and 6. The reasons are complex – and subject to heated debate among linguists – but the theory is this: the better children are at detecting syllables, rhymes and phonemes at an early age, the quicker and more successful their progress with reading. Familiarity with nursery rhymes appears to help. They have an educational value we still don't entirely understand."

Phonemes are small units of speech which distinguish one word from another, for example 'p', 'b', 'd' and 't' in the English words 'pad, pat, bad and bat'. They are at the centre of the debate over the usefulness of nursery rhymes in teaching children to read. As Laurie J Harper put it in *The Journal of Language and Literary Education* (2011): "Phonological awareness is an important precursor to learning to read. This awareness of phonemes fosters a child's ability to hear and blend sounds, encode and decode words, and to spell phonetically." Frances James, author of *The*

Cambridge Book of Nursery Rhymes (1996) found that nearly 500 simple words can be derived by reciting only 37 nursery rhymes including introductions to words ending in 'ash', 'eat', 'ick', 'op' and 'ump'.

This is in line with the original intention of the earliest nursery rhyme books. A copy of *The Pretty Book*, published in the 1780s, can be found in the Osborne Collection in the Toronto Public Library. Its mission statement is proudly set out on page 3: "A little play book for all pretty masters and misses to teach children their letters as soon as they can speak." And an advertisement on page 64, the last page of the oldest surviving nursery rhyme book in the world (*Tommy Thumb's Pretty Song Book Vol II*), ends with a poetic advertisement from Nurse Lovechild:

> *The Child's Plaything*
> *I recommend for Cheating*
> *Children into Learning*
> *Without any Beating.*

It took another 240 years for the research to start to see if there were indeed links between chanting nursery rhymes and improved language development. The earliest findings usually cited were by Peter Bryant, Lynette Bradley and Morag Maclean of Oxford University. Their first study in 1987 of 66 children aged three to six found a strong highly specific relationship between their knowledge of nursery rhymes and their ability to recognize words after 15 months. Their second study involving 64 children found a similar link after three years with success in spelling tests. Both these findings allowed for differences in social backgrounds, IQs and the children's phonological skills at the start of the project.

It was possibly these studies which caused Mem Fox, the Australian author and educationalist specialising in literacy, to write in her 2001 book *Reading Magic*: "Experts in literacy and child development have discovered that if children know eight nursery rhymes by heart by the time they're four years old, they're usually the best readers by the time they are eight."

When I approached Mem Fox in 2023 for further details about this research I was told: "The origin of the statistic you asked about is now lost in the mists of time. I heard it at an international literary conference in South Africa about 25 years ago." Pity – because this is just the kind of pithy finding which would have encapsulated in a short paragraph the importance of learning nursery rhymes.

In June 2019 Professor Usha Goswami, Director of the Centre for Neuroscience in Education at Cambridge University, described to *The Times Educational Supplement* how nursery rhymes helped to kick-start children's developing language systems and helped pupils with dyslexia. She was later part of a combined research team that looked at 50 infants aged four months, seven and 11 months, as they watched a video of a teacher singing 18 nursery rhymes to an infant. Their conclusions in the journal *Nature Communications* found that in their first few months babies learn to talk from rhythmic rather than phonetic information.

Professor Goswami has also been involved in two further studies published by Frontiers in Education in 2020 and 2021 looking at the effectiveness of GraphoGame Rime, a computer software programme teaching reading, which encourages and checks children's ability to match words with rhyme. The research among nearly 400 six-to-seven-year-olds in 15 primary schools revealed benefits for struggling readers and other disadvantaged children particularly boys from a programme which was found by both teachers and children easy to use and fun.

As computer games and mobile apps may be responsible for turning families away from nursery rhymes it's only common sense that they should be used in their defence.

The largest and most comprehensive study I could find exploring the effectiveness of nursery rhymes in improving language development and skills was carried out by CELL, an American organisation dedicated to exploring evidence of ways of improving early literacy. In 2011 this Center for Early Literacy Learning published a paper looking at the relationship between young children's nursery rhyme experiences and knowledge and phonological and print-related abilities. Funded by the US Department of Education, it covered nearly 5,300 children aged three to six in 14 studies. It too found that nursery rhyme awareness contributed to increased reading skills regardless of the children's age or 'developmental condition'. Nursery rhymes benefited children with or without disabilities but the authors (Carl J Dunst, Diana Meter and Deborah W. Hamby) went on: "Especially noteworthy is the fact that nursery rhyme experiences and knowledge were most strongly related to the literacy outcomes among children with identified disabilities." For these children nursery rhyme games and activities were "especially important".

In a separate paper Dr Dunst, one of the American researchers and an author of several books on literacy, found that middle class children had a better knowledge of nursery rhymes and learned nursery rhymes at a faster rate through their pre-school years than children from working class families. Any decline in nursery rhyme chanting could therefore be a social mobility issue as well as one for countering disabilities.

In the same paper Carl Dunst observed: "It is surprising that so few studies of young children's nursery rhyme knowledge have been conducted given the fact that nursery rhymes have been such an important part of children's upbringing for centuries." Later he wrote: "Our knowledge of the development of nursery rhyme knowledge is quite limited" and he called for further investigation.

More research into the value of nursery rhymes is necessary but this will take money and time – and if nursery rhymes are on the decline then something should be done in the immediate future to revive them. Work should start now while at least half of the nation's parenthood appears to use and enjoy them.

There is no actual centre for the propagation of nursery rhymes and no educational organisation co-ordinating research into their effectiveness and surveys into their relevance among today's young families. Could a museum, library or art centre link with a research organisation in Britain, America, Canada or elsewhere.

Google 'nurseryrhymes.com' and you come across a website offering free lyrics and music to nursery rhymes "that have been passed down through the ages". This is a great resource for over 500 nursery rhymes and songs which can be accessed alphabetically and by genre (e.g. king and queen songs, riddle songs or tongue twisters) with access to colouring pages, games, and videos.

NurseryRhymes.com says it attracts millions of surfing visitors a year. Could this modern equivalent of the short-lived 19th century Percy Society, which would be widely accessible and promoted in our centre, not be expanded to include research into the meaning of nursery rhymes and into their usefulness and declining usage?

Next on my Google list is the admirable World Nursery Rhyme Week. Five different nursery rhymes are chosen each year for schools, nurseries and playgroups to celebrate by singing them during one week in November. It was founded as National Nursery Rhyme Week in 2003 by Claire Bennett, Managing Director of Music Bugs, which organises sensory music classes for babies, toddlers and pre-schoolers. It soon became worldwide with growing interest from abroad. Numbers taking part have grown impressively. Claire recorded in November 2023 that the week had attracted 731,189 children across 92 countries - the highest number of participants ever.

It shows that a proactive event can widen interest in nursery rhymes among teachers and their young charges and their families. But this is just one week in a year. Something in addition and more permanent is needed to keep nursery rhymes alive. Every week should be a nursery rhyme week.

A centre for the propagation of nursery rhymes could celebrate their bygone use in so many different ways. It could start small and would have shelves and display cases of old books of nursery rhymes or replicas of them and later books of nursery rhymes from all quarters of the world. It could collect works of fiction and faction that have nursery rhymes in them, especially those which include them in their titles.

Agatha Christie used them to sew threads through the fabric of some of her detective novels. Along with *Three Blind Mice*, as described above, she also wrote: *One, Two Buckle my Shoe* (1940), *Five Little Pigs* (1942), *Crooked House* (1949), *A Pocketful of Rye* (1953), and *Hickory Dickory Dock* (1955).

The prolific bestselling American writer James Patterson has written nearly 400 books. Over 30 years between 1979 and 2005 he often used nursery rhymes for their titles: *See How They Run* (1979), *Cradle and All* (1980), *Along Came a Spider* (1993), *Kiss the Girls* (1995), and *Jack and Jill* (1996). *Pop Goes the Weasel* in 1999 was followed by *Roses are Red* (2000), *Violets are Blue* (2001) *Four Blind Mice* (2002), *London Bridges* (2004) and *Mary, Mary* (2005).

Our centre could have a games corner: *Little Jack Horner* was a game like *Happy Families* introduced by Mcloughlin Brothers of New York around 1888. Plums of various kinds pictured on cards were pulled from the pack on the table and were used by players to form complete sets. Around the same time De La Rue's *Little*

Jack Horner Snap came in a pack with 13 different nursery rhymes each with four cards. Our centre should also include some of the games, songs and children's work in the Opie collections at the British and Bodleian Libraries if their curators were prepared to share them.

The centre could resound to nursery rhyme music and not just from an old gramophone player blaring out *Old MacDonald had a Farm* which I heard many times in my youth. But there could be pop songs too as pop songs and nursery rhymes have been closely intertwined. The BBC Radio series *Pop Goes the Beatles* featured songs from the four lads who became international stars. It was broadcast weekly on the Light Programme between June 4th and September 24th 1963. Each of the 15 episodes began and ended with a rock'n roll version of *Pop Goes the Weasel*. The centre could also play *Lavender Blue* from Kenneth Branagh's 2015 romantic fantasy film version of *Cinderella*. And it could even play an excerpt from Act 1 of Benjamin's Britten's opera *The Turn of the Screw* where the frightened governess is put at ease by the children singing *Tom, Tom, the Piper's Son*.

Space could later be reserved in its art gallery for the representations of the most beautiful pictures by Kate Greenaway, Arthur Rackham, Randolph Caldecott, Dorothy Wheeler and other famous nursery rhyme illustrators including John Tenniel's illustration of *Humpty Dumpty* and John Everett Millais's portrayal of *Little Miss Muffet*. And, of course, a special section would be found for the series of paintings and prints which the Portuguese artist Paula Rego began in 1991 when she was the first Associate Artist at the National Gallery in London. Humorous and haunting, 26 illustrated rhymes were published in 1994 with an introduction by the writer Marina Warner who said the artist had "seized hold of Mother Goose, the magnificent body of oral literature, and transformed her through private memory and imagination."

There could be another area too for famous cartoons which can be found in the *Oxford Dictionary of Nursery Rhymes*. Computer stations could abound with games to help children draw nursery rhymes inspired by these pictures.

A large dressing-up cupboard full of clothes could store nursery rhyme costumes to hire out for children's parties, pantomimes and other performances. From this might emerge a commercial centre selling Doulton china nursery rhyme figurines, tee-shirts and mugs as well as those vintage breakfast bowls with nursery rhyme figures appearing at the bottom when the porridge is almost eaten!

And wouldn't it be lovely if the opening of this centre could be publicised by the unveiling of a life-size tableau of a famous nursery rhyme made by young children? An exhibition centre might inspire villages, towns and cities to celebrate a nursery rhyme with pageants and parades. These cities, towns, villages and other places would be recorded on a new Nursery Rhyme Map of Britain. In my two books on nursery rhymes I have come across the following:

March: St Clement Danes Church, London: on the first Thursday in March St Clements holds a special *Oranges and Lemons* day service.

May 1st: National Mother Goose Day – celebrated in America since 1987.

May: Faringdon, Oxfordshire: *Sing a Song of Sixpence* is commemorated by 'Blackbird Day'. Residents bake pies to celebrate the rhyme which was used to make fun of one of their famous citizens Henry James Pye, Poet Laureate from 1790 until his death in 1819.

August: Eyam, Derbyshire: The Derbyshire Peak District village of Eyam still remembers *Ring a Ring o'Roses* on Plague Sunday on the last Sunday in August. A wreath of roses is laid on Catherine Mompesson's grave in the churchyard of St Lawrence's even though as I show in my first book this joyful rhyme is not actually connected with death and disease.

October: Banbury: Banbury's Hobby Horse Festival takes place on the second Saturday of October. The town is overrun with 'unusual equines' in a parade of beasts celebrating *Ride a Cock Horse to Banbury Cross*.

November: Third week is World Nursery Rhyme Week as described above.

But more places could be added just from the nursery rhymes that I have studied. Here are some possible dates:

April 9th: Royal Theatre, Haymarket, or Eagle Tavern, City Road, London could be *Pop Goes the Weasel Day*. *The Extravaganzas of J.R. Planché* took place on Easter April 9th 1855 and was attended by many famous London impresarios. A new version of *Pop Goes the Weasel* was performed which featured the Eagle Tavern in City Road, London.

April 30th: Hampton Court: The birth date of Mary II, Queen of England, a keen gardener who imported many exotic plants to the gardens of this palace. It would be fitting to have a Spring garden *Mary, Mary Quite Contrary* festival linking her to the nursery rhyme and commemorating her gardening skills.

May 15: Dover: the date and place where bad King John fell down and surrendered his crown and kingdom to the papal legate at Ewell near Dover. This may be the origin of *Jack and Jill* as Jill may have started life as a man called Gill!

May 18th: York: on that day the *Grand Old Duke of York*, Frederick, 12th Duke of York, suffered a defeat at the Battle of Tourcoing in Flanders, in 1794.

June 8th or 9th: Gloucester Cathedral: *Dr Foster*, alias Dr Brent, *went to Gloucester* on June 8th and 9th 1635 and may or may not have got stuck in a puddle! The cathedral could celebrate one of its most famous former visitors.

August 22nd: Edinburgh: On August 22nd King George IV was attended by 457 ladies in the drawing rooms of Holyrood Palace. The custom required that he kiss each of them on the cheek. This could celebrate one theory for the origins of *Georgie Porgie*.

September 3rd: Worcester: the best date to celebrate *The Lion and the Unicorn* where the Scottish troops were driven 'round the town' at the Battle of Worcester in 1651 where Oliver Cromwell (the lion) defeated a largely Scottish force under Prince Charles (later Charles II) the unicorn.

September 8th: Colchester: ' For t'was my Lady's Birthday' is a line in the rhyme dating *Old King Cole* who reigned from Colchester and died in 297. September 8th is the day on which the birthday of the Virgin Mary is celebrated.

September 8th: London Bridge. Also on this day in 1014 the English celebrated a famous victory led by Ethelred the Unready when his Norwegian ally pulled down the bridge and stopped the Vikings overrunning London.

280 years ago Mary Cooper was running a bookshop in Paternoster Row near St Paul's Cathedral, London, when she had the bright idea of publishing a small collection of nursery rhymes under the title: *Tom Thumb's Pretty Song Book* which was dedicated to a fictitious Nurse Lovechild. According to Andrea Immel

and Brian Alderson in their book *Nurse Lovechild's Legacy* this volume was first advertised in London's *Daily Gazeteer*, also in Paternoster Row, on March 14th 1744.

From this one publication grew the birth and spread of the nursery rhyme across the world. I would call the new centre: 'The Mary Cooper Centre for Nursery Rhymes'. Let's hope it's up and running by March 14th 2044 so we can celebrate the 300th anniversary of the oldest surviving book of nursery rhymes and the extraordinary foresight and business acumen of this remarkable widow.

Clues to the illustrations for the 14 nursery rhymes in this book.

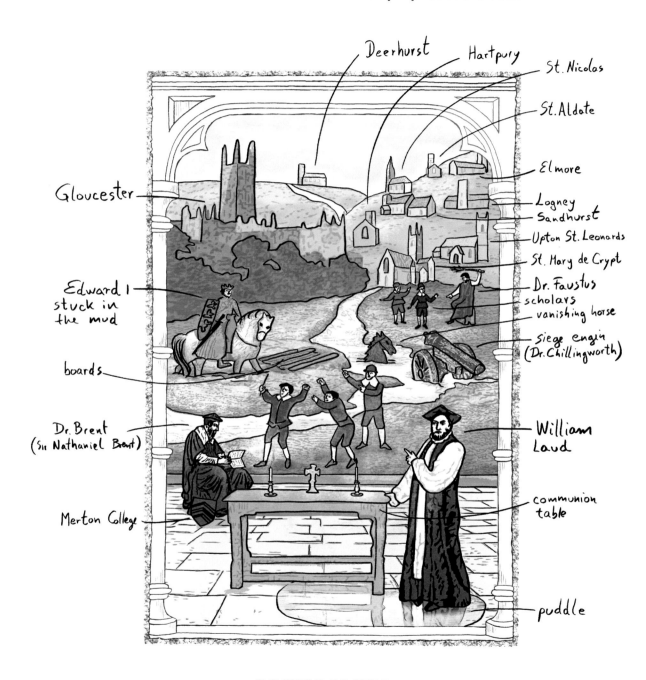

DOCTOR FOSTER

CLUES TO THE ILLUSTRATIONS | 163

GOOSEY, GOOSEY, GANDER

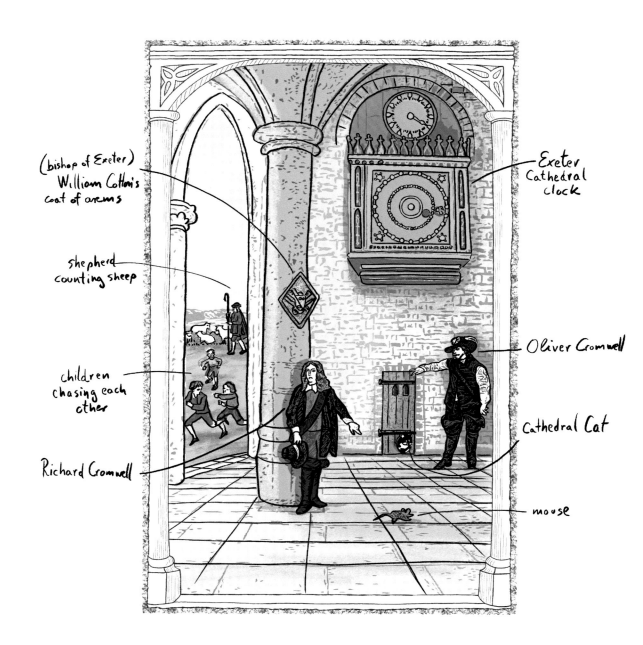

HICKORY DICKORY DOCK

CLUES TO THE ILLUSTRATIONS | 165

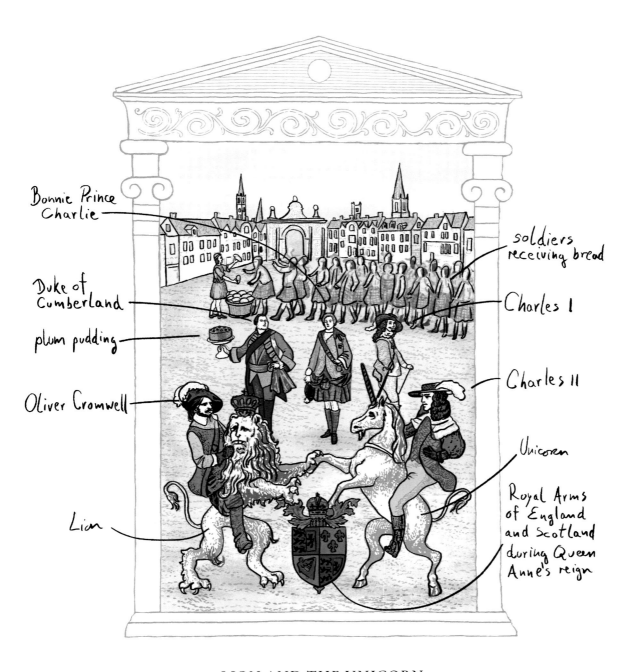

LION AND THE UNICORN

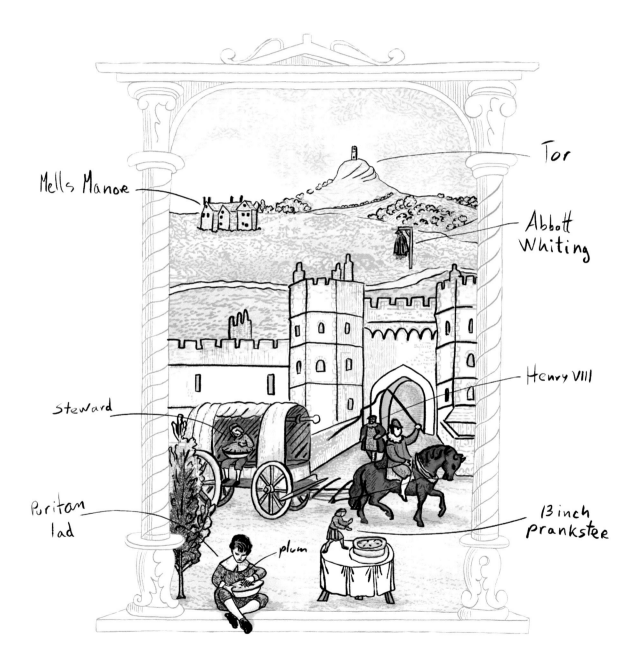

LITTLE JACK HORNER

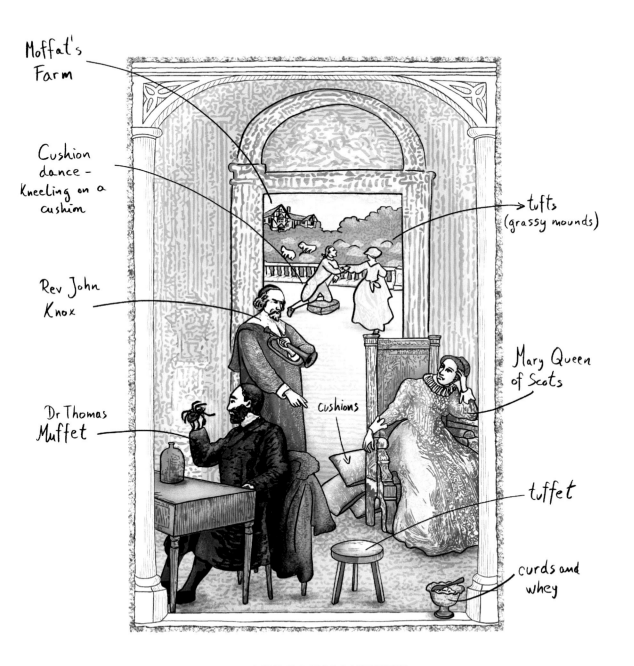

LITTLE MISS MUFFET

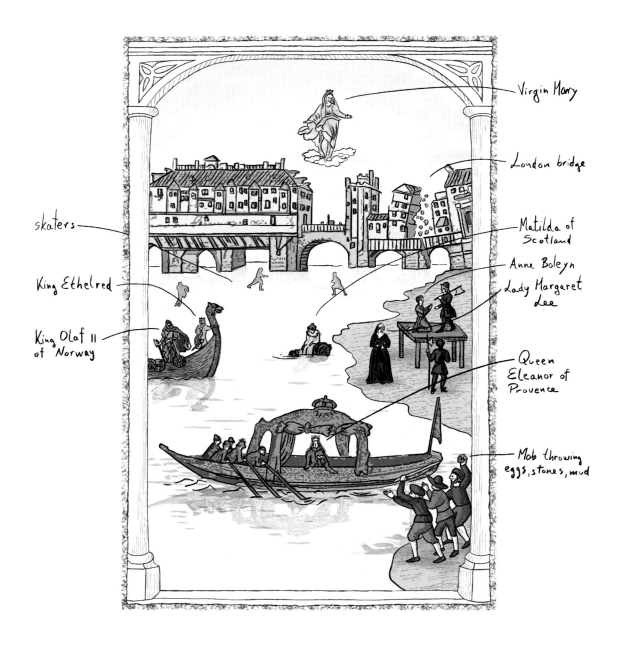

LONDON BRIDGE

CLUES TO THE ILLUSTRATIONS | 169

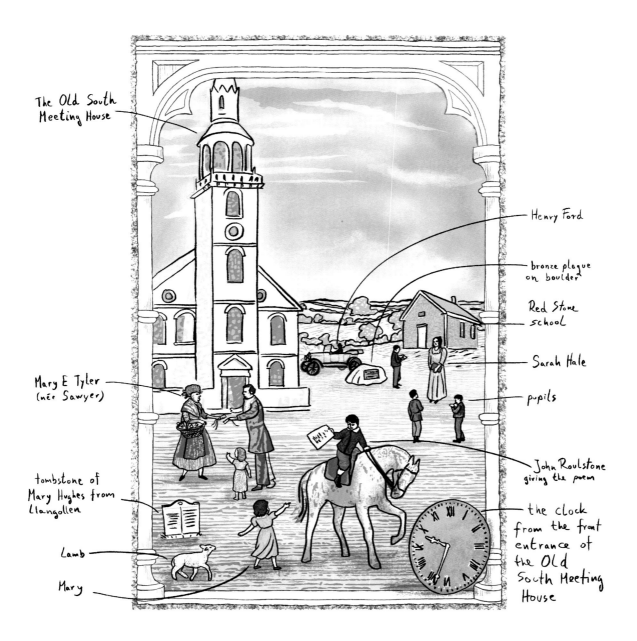

MARY HAD A LITTLE LAMB

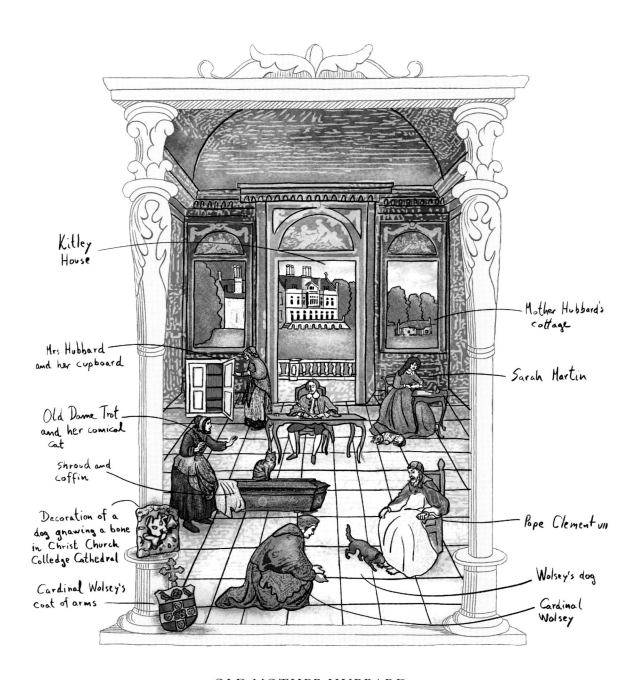

OLD MOTHER HUBBARD

CLUES TO THE ILLUSTRATIONS | 171

POP GOES THE WEASEL

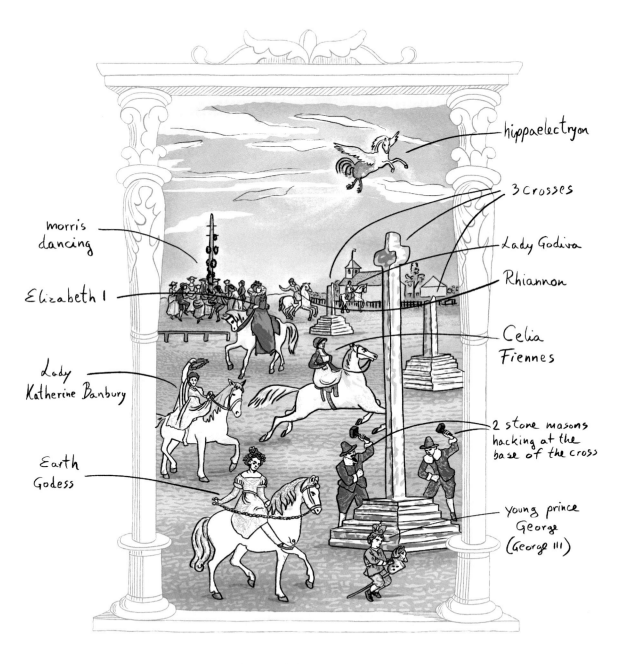

RIDE A COCK HORSE

CLUES TO THE ILLUSTRATIONS | 173

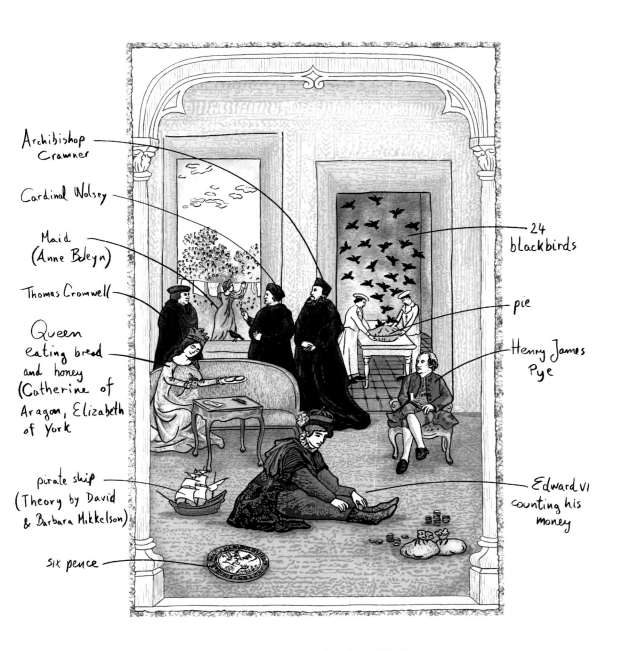

SING A SONG OF SIXPENCE

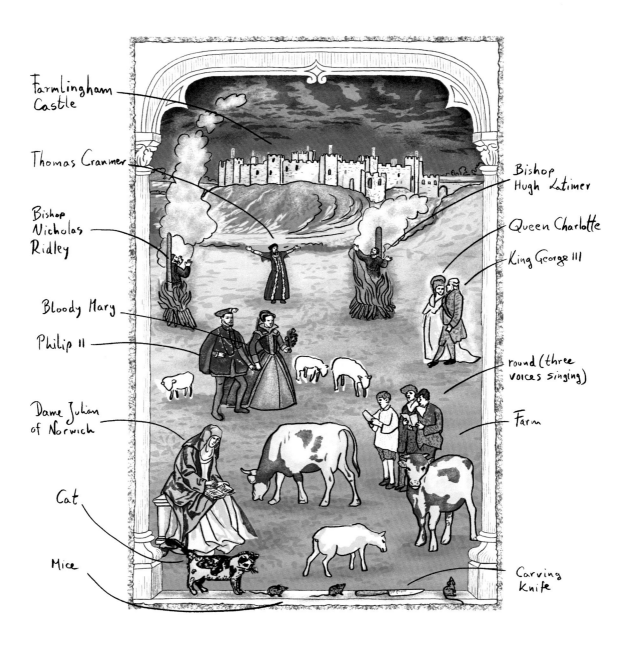

THREE BLIND MICE

CLUES TO THE ILLUSTRATIONS | 175

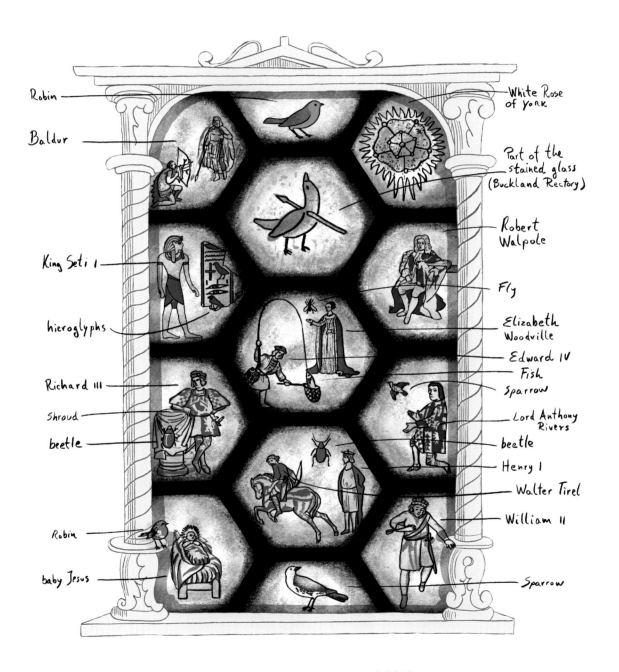

WHO KILLED COCK ROBIN?

Index of People and Places

Aesop, 44, 151
Agesilaus, 111
Akanthos, Greece, 44
Albert, Prince, 101, 116
Alchin, Linda, 33, 41, 63, 79, 125, 132
Alcott, Louisa, 85
Alderson, Brian, 120, 160
Alençon, Duc d', 96
Anjou, Geoffrey of, 44
Anne, Princess, 118-119, 120
Anne, Queen, 45
Anne, Queen of Bohemia, 116
Anselm, Archbishop of Canterbury, 144
Antwerp, 59
Aprice, John, 133
Aquitaine, 44
Aragon, 56, 93, 124. 132
Aristophanes, 110
Arnopp, Judith, 125
Arthur, King, 44, 119
Arnold, Samuel, 30-31
Ashdown, Margaret, 78
Ashley, Ralph, Father, 33
Asquith, Katharine, 57, 61
Asquith, Raymond, 51, 57-61, 148
Atkin, Malcolm, 47
Azem, Sabry Adel, 145

Baker, Richard, 132
Balliol College, Oxford, 131
Banbury, Oxfordshire, 109-119, 158
Banbury, Amy, 115
Banbury, Katherine & Jonathan, 115, 118
Baring-Gould, William & Ceil, 14, 97
Basel, 65
Bastard, John Pollexfen, 97, 98
Bath, 58
Baxter, Richard, 47
Beard, Roger, 152

Beaton, Cardinal David, 31, 32, 34
Beaumont, Francis, 128
Becket, Thomas, 56, 80
Beesley, Alfred, 112
Bennett, Claire, 156
Berkshire, 10
Bertha, Queen, 9, 11
Bett, Henry, 14, 75
Birmingham, 102, 110
Bishop, Samuel, 55
Blackbeard, Captain, 127
Bland, Rev Michael, 143
Blows, Alice, 60
Boadicea, Queen, 127
Bocardo Prison, Oxford, 131
Bodleian Library, Oxford, 45, 53, 64, 132, 157. 185
Bohemia, 116
Boleyn, Anne, 79, 93, 124-125, 132
Bond St, London, 64
Borrowdale, Cumbria, 41
Boston, Massachusetts, 7, 8, 9, 84-85, 87, 89
Boswell, James, 135-136
Bow Bridge, London, 79
Boyle, John, 58
Bradley, Lynette, 153
Brain, Jessica, 44-45
Branagh, Kenneth, 157
Brathwait, Richard, 113
Brent, Nathaniel, 22-23, 24, 26, 159
Breverton, Terry, 124
Brewer, Cobham, 116-117, 118
Bristol, 8
British Library, London, 12, 30, 52. 101, 111, 129, 184
British Museum, London, 19
British Ornithological Trust, 118
Britten, Benjamin, 157
Broad St, Oxford, 131

Broadwater Cemetery, Worthing, 88
Brookmans Park, 67, 68
Broughton Castle, Banbury, 115,
Brown Philip, 22-24,
Browne, Catherine, 68
Bruges, 59, 60
Bryant, Peter, 153
Buckingham Palace, 102
Buckinghamshire, 38
Buckland Rectory, Glos, 140, 141, 143
Bullock, Collin, 15
Bunker Hill, Boston, Mass, 87
Burne-Jones, Edward, 57
Burton, Robert, 111
Bute, Lord, 136

Caldecott, Randolph, 157
California, 134
Calne, Wilts, 68
Cambridge, 4, 65, 68, 116, 153, 154
Canterbury, 22, 24, 34, 96, 132, 144
Capen, Rev Lemuel, 86, 69
Capitol Hill, Rome, 32
Caractacus, 127
Carey, Henry, 12, 51, 54, 76, 119-120
Carlisle, 46
Carnan, Thomas, 10
Carroll, Lewis, 45
Carson, Annette, 142
Carter, William, 68
Catherine of Aragon, 56, 93, 124, 132
Chantilly, Château de, 118
Charles I, 18, 22, 46, 47
Charles II, 37, 47, 54, 77
Charlestown, Mass., 8
Charlie, Bonnie Prince, 46
Charlotte, Queen of Mecklenburg-Strelitz, 135
Charterhouse Manor, 59

INDEX OF PEOPLE AND PLACES | 177

Chaucer, Geoffrey, 96
Chillingworth, Dr William, 18
Christ Church College, Oxford, 94
Christie, Agatha, 58, 151, 156
Churchyard, Thomas, 94
City Road, London, 103, 104, 158
Clark, John, 75, 78
Clarke, John, 38
Clement VII, 93
Cloford, Somerset, 58, 59
Cock Horse Inn, Detling, Kent, 110
Colchester, 159
Cole, King, 159
Columbus, Christopher, 39
Connolly, Sharon, 135
Conquest, Benjamin, 103
Conway, David, 103
Cooper, Mary, 12, 76, 140, 159, 160
Cooper, Trevor, 24, 25
Corbet, Richard, 113
Cork, Countess of, 57-58
Cornhill, Banbury, 112
Cornmarket, Oxford, 131
Cotswolds, 114
Cotton, Bishop William, 39
Coulon, Eugène, 102
Covent Garden, London, 11
Coventry, 115, 117
Cromwell, Oliver, 33, 37, 46, 47, 48
Cromwell, Richard, 37, 38
Cromwell, Thomas, 125
Crouch Hill, Banbury, 111
Crowninshield, Edward, 11
Culloden, 46
Cumberland, Duke of, 46
Cumbria, 41

Daube, David, 14, 18, 19, 116, 118
Deacon-Davis, Chris, 141

Deerhurst, Glos, 23-26
Delamar, Gloria, 9, 10, 14
Delaney, Lesley Jane, 96-97
Denbighshire, 88
Derby, 46, 133
Derbyshire, 133, 158
Detling, Kent, 110
Devlin, Angela, 184
Devlin, Cyra, 124
Devlin, Daniel, 184
Devon, 39, 97
Devonshire, 97
Douce, Francis, 19
Doulting, Somerset, 58
Dover, 110, 159
Downey, Catherine, 129
Dragoslavić, Katarina, 184
Drake, Francis, 65
Drowry, Thomas, 133
Dunbar, 48
Dunkirk, 48
Dunning, Robert, 60
Dunst, Carl, 154-155
Durham, 102

Eagle Tavern, London, 103-104, 158
Eckenstein, Lina, 14, 66, 67, 96, 145, 146
Edinburgh, 39, 40, 63, 64, 159
Edison, Thomas, 84
Edward I, 17, 18, 80, 81
Edward IV, 141, 142, 143, 144
Edward V, 142
Edward VI, 34, 128, 129, 132
Eglinton, Lord, 135-136
Eleanor, Queen of Provence, 80, 81
Eliot, John Fleet, 9, 11
Elizabeth I, 24, 32, 96, 109, 110, 117, 118, 132

Elizabeth of York, Queen, 125
Elyot, Thomas, 111
Emerson, Ralph
Essex, 37, 79
Essex, Earl of, 65
Ethelred (the Unready), 77, 78, 159
Evans, T, 95
Eward, Suzanne, 20, 21
Ewell, Kent, 159
Exeter Cathedral, 38, 39
Eyam, Derbyshire, 158

Faringdon, Oxon, 158
Felsted School, 37
Ferguson, Diana, 15, 63, 124
Fielding, Henry, 54
Fiennes, Celia, 115, 118
Fiennes, Joseph & Ralph, 115
Fiennes, W.E. Blake, 115
Fiennes, William, 115
Fife, Scotland, 31
Flanders, 159
Fleet, Elizabeth, 8, 9
Fleet, Thomas, 9, 11
Fletcher, John, 127
Florence, 125
Florida, 135
Ford, Henry, 88, 89
Fox, Mem, 153-154
Foxe, John, 93, 132-133
Fowle, Jonathan, 39
Frances, Henry, 32
Francis II, 63
Franklin, Benjamin, 11
Fraser, Antonia, 63-64
Frederick, Duke of York, 159
Frome, Somerset, 59
Fulchred, Abbot of Féez, 143-144

INDEX OF PEOPLE AND PLACES

Gardiner, Samuel Rawson, 47
Gardiner, Stephen, Bishop, 32, 132
Garnet, Henry, 33
George II, 46, 77
George III, 120, 126, 135
George IV, 159,
Ghent, 59
Gibbs, Laura, 44
Gladstone, William & Herbert, 111
Glastonbury, 38, 55-60
Glastonbury Tor, 56
Gloucester, 17-18, 19-25, 144, 159
Gloucestershire, 17, 22, 24, 140, 142
Gloucester Cathedral, 20, 21, 159
Godiva, Lady, 115, 117
Gomme, Alice, 74-78
Gomme, George, Laurence, 75
Goose, Elizabeth Foster, 8-9, 11
Goose, Isaac, 7-8
Goose, Mary, 7-8
Goswami, Usha, 154
Granary Burial Ground, Boston, Mass., 7-8,
Greaves, Paul, 39
Grey, Lady Jane, 132
Green M, 77
Green, Percy B, 14, 40, 53-54, 61, 111
Greenaway, Kate, 157
Gregory V, 9
Griffiths, Martin, 147
Grimaldi, Joseph, 11
Grimsbury, Oxon, 113
Guinevere, Queen, 119, 120

Habington, Thomas & Mary, 33
Hackney, London, 103
Hake, Edward, 32
Hale, Frances, 89
Hale, Horatio, 88-89

Hale, Sarah Josepha, 87-90
Halliwell, James Orchard, 13, 14, 17, 19, 20, 40, 53, 95, 111, 124, 127, 128, 135, 136
Hamby, Dorothy, 154
Hampshire, 144
Hampton Court, 159
Hardy, Sarah, 97
Hare, Michael, 24-26
Harper, Laurie J, 152
Harradine, Eunice, 115
Harris, John, 94, 146
Harrowven, Jean, 14, 126, 143, 144
Harvard University, 56, 90
Harvey, Paul, 112
Hause, Prof Earl Malcolm, 38
Henri IV, 125
Henry I, 44, 79, 144
Henry III, 80, 81
Henry VII, 125, 128
Henry VIII, 51, 55, 56, 58, 59, 68, 93, 124, 125, 128, 132
Herbert, Mary Countess, 65
Hertfordshire, 79, 141
Heywood, John, 129
Hibbard, Ruth, 116
Hindlip Hall, Worcs, 33
Holmes, Oliver 85
Holyrood Palace, Edinburgh, 63, 64, 159
Horner, Frances, 57, 61
Horner, Jack, 10, 12, 51-61, 148, 156-157,
Horner, John, 57,
Horner, Strangways, Mrs, 58
Horner, Robert, 60
Horner, Thomas, 55-57, 59, 60
Houliston, Victor, 65
Hoxton, London, 103
Hughes, Mary, 88

Huntingdon, Henry of, 143-144
Huntington, Robert, 25
Hussey, Christopher, 97
Hutchings, J, 114
Hutton, William Holden, 22

Iles, Norman, 135
Immel, Andrea, 120, 159, 184
Ipswich, 68, 102

Jack, Albert, 15, 32, 37, 46, 65, 76, 89-90, 115, 132
James I, 20, 45, 101
James, Frances, 152-153
James, Owen, 129
John (King), 159
Johnson, Samuel, 114
Jones, John, 21
Jonson, Ben, 112
Julian, Dame of Norwich, 133-135
Jurassic Way, 111

Kent, 44, 110
Ker, John Bellenden, 13, 14
Keswick, Cumbria, 41
Kidderminster, 47,
Killick, Bill, 68
Kimball, Polly, 86, 89
King, William, 45
King's College, London, 135
Kitley House, Yealmpton, Devon, 97-98
Knight, Matthew, 113
Knollys, William, 118
Knox, John, 31-32, 63-64
Kytson, Thomas, 60

Laing, Samuel, 77-78
Lamb, Charles, 126
Lambeth Palace, 24, 80

Lang, Andrew, 9
Latimer, Hugh, Bishop, 121, 133, 134
Laud, William, Archbishop, 20-22, 23, 24, 25
Leavis, F. R., 84
Lee, Margaret, 79
Leeke, Brian & Jean, 26
Leicester, 47
Leigh, Lady, 78
Leigh-on-Mendip, Somerset, 58, 60
Leofric, Earl of Mercia, 117
Leong, Sandy, 15, 33, 65, 93, 125, 132
Lewis, Elizabeth, 133
Leyland, John, 59, 112
Library of Congress, Washington DC, 102
Lille, 143
Lincoln, 112
Lincoln, Abraham, 87
Livy, Titus, 32
Llangollen, 88
Loe, William, 20
London, 7, 10, 24, 30, 47, 53, 54, 55, 56, 57, 58, 59, 64, 65, 67, 68, 71-81, 102, 103, 105, 111, 114, 116, 132, 133, 135, 143, 151, 157, 158, 159, 160
London Bridge, 12, 13, 32, 71-81, 156, 159
London Library, 184
London University, 135, 152
Longfellow, 85
Loret, Jean, 9
Louis XI, 143
Luxor, 145

MacCulloch, Diarmaid, 34
Maclean, Hugh, 23, 25, 26
Maclean, Morag, 153
Maidstone, 110, 133
Malmesbury, William of, 144

Malory, Thomas, 119
Mancini, Domenico, 143
Mandale, W.R., 103, 106
Marlowe, Christopher, 19, 110
Marmentier, Jean de, 44
Martial, Marcus, 39
Martin, Sarah Catherine, 94-97
Mary I, 32, 34, 131-133
Mary II, 159
Mary Queen of Scots, 63-64
Mason, Lowell, 89
Massachusetts, 7, 8, 11, 85, 87-88, 119, 140
Matilda, Queen of Scotland, 79
Maxse, Lady, 1, 7, 13, 125
McCanlis, Patrick, 141
McGuffey, William, 87
Mecklenberg, 135, 145
Medici, Marie de, 125
Mee, Arthur, 24
Mells Manor, Somerset, 51, 55, 57-60
Mendips, 51, 59, 60
Merchant Taylor's School, London, 65
Merton College, Oxford, 22, 24
Meter, Diana, 154-155
Middlesex, 79
Middlesex, Mass., 88
Mikkelson, David & Barbara, 127
Millais, John Everett, 157
Miller, David, 115, 118
Moffat, William, 68
Moffat's Lane, 67-68
Monmouth, Geoffrey of, 53
Mompesson, Catherine, 158
Montfort, Simon de, 18, 81
Montgomerie, Alexander, 135-136
Montgomery, William Henry, 101-102
Moore, Susan, 125
Morris, Will, 26

Morrison, Julia, 31
Mortimer's Cross, Herts, 141
Muffet, Jane, 68
Muffet, Patience, 68, 157
Muffet, Thomas, 63-68
Musée Condé, Chantille, 118
Museum of London, 75

Naseby, Battle of, 46-47
Nettelhorst, Robin P, 134
Newbery, John, 10, 53
Newbury, Berks, 19
Newcastle, 102
New College, Oxford, 115, 140
New Forest, Hants, 144
New Hampshire, USA, 87, 88, 89
Newport, USA, 89
New York, 137, 156
Nichols, John, 117-118
Normandy, 44
Northall, G. F. 14, 60,
North Mymms, Herts, 67-68
Norwich, 133-135

Ogilvy, Marion, 31
Oklahoma, 44
Olaf II, 77
Oldcorne, Edward, 33
Old Rectory, Buckland, 141
Old South Meeting House, Boston, Mass., 84-85
Oliphant, Thomas, 136
Opie, Peter & Iona, 11, 13, 14, 17, 30, 41, 43, 45, 46, 52, 56, 60, 74, 76, 77, 97, 101, 103, 105, 106, 114, 116, 118, 126, 135
Orrery, 57-58
Ottar, the Black, 78
Oxford, 4, 14, 18, 20, 22, 24, 32, 44, 45, 46, 94, 104, 112, 115, 116, 119, 131, 138, 140, 152, 153

Oxford, Lord (see Asquith),
Oxfordshire, 109, 136, 158
Owen, Nicholas, 33

Paracelsus, 65
Paris, 102
Paternoster Row, London, 159
Patterson, James, 156
Pavilion Theatre, London, 103
Peacock, Thomas Love, 55
Peel, Albert, 59
Peloponnese, 75
Penny, Thomas, 65
Percy, Henry, 125
Perrault, Charles, 9
Pevsner, Nikolaus, 38
Philadelphia, 11
Philip II, 132
Philips, Ambrose, 12, 51
Phillips, Rebecca, 21
Pierce, Patricia, 32, 73, 75, 77, 81
Pilgrims Way, 110
Pitti Palace, Florence, 125
Pittsburg, 127
Planché, James, 103, 158
Playford, John, 66
Pliny, Gaius, 66
Pope, Alexander, 12
Potts, William, 111, 112, 114, 118, 119
Preston Pans, Battle of, 46
Prosser, Percival, 104
Prynne, William, 22
Pudding Lane, Boston, Mass., 8, 9
Pye, Henry, 126, 158

Quartz Hill, California, 134
Queenhithe, London, 80

Rackham, Arthur, 157

Raleigh, Walter, 76
Ravenscroft, Thomas, 133, 135
Reading, Berks, 10
Reedman, J. P., 81
Rego, Paula, 157
Revere, Paul, 7
Reynolds, K.D, 57
Rhiannon, (goddess), 114
Richard I, 44
Richard II, 116
Richard III, 142-143
Richard, Duke of York, 125
Ridley, Nicholas, Bishop, 131, 132, 133, 134
Ritson, Joseph, 20, 29, 128
Rivers, Lord Anthony, 142
Rivers, Rev Anthony, 113
Robert II (of France), 9
Roberts, Chris, 14, 133, 146
Robinson, John Martin, 44
Rochester, 44, 80
Rogers, Sherbrooke, 87
Rome, 32, 93
Rosselli, Giovanni de, 124
Roud, Steve, 29
Roulstone, John, 86-90
Rowlatt-Jones, W Roger, 110
Royal Holloway College, 102

St Andrew's Castle, Fife, 31
St Clement Danes Church, London, 158
St David's, Wales, 22
St Lawrence's Church, Eyam, 158
St Mary's Priory, Deerhurst, 23-26
St Michael's, Gloucester, 21, 141
St Paul's Cathedral, London, 159
Salih, Sarah, 135
Samber, Robert, 10
Sawyer, Francis, 90

Sawyer, Mary (née Tyler), 85-90
Sawyer, Nat, 86
Séez, Abbot of, 143-144
Selwodde, Abbate, 59
Selwood, Dominic, 47
Seti I, King, 145
Sheppey, 44
Shepton Mallet, Somerset, 58
Shewell, Henry, 113
Shoreditch, London, 65, 102
Shrewsbury, Abbot of, 143
Sidney, Philip, 65
Simpson, Jacqueline, 29
Sloman, Charles, 103
Smith, Elmer Boyd, 14, 17
Smith, Miles, 20-21
Socrates, 111
Soho Sq, London, 102
Somerset, 51, 56, 57, 58, 59, 60, 148
Sonnichsen, Sandra, 89
Southwark, London, 32, 77, 80
Spence, Lewis, 14, 74
Spencer, Charles, 144
Spenser, Edward, 44, 96
Spitalfields, London, 26,
Stanmore Hill, Banbury, 110
Star Chamber, 113
Steevens, George, 126
Sterling, Mass., 85, 88
Stevens, Albert Mason, 14, 32, 47
Stirling, 105
Stoneleigh Park, Warwicks, 78
Stow, John, 80
Stratford, London, 79, 133
Strickland, Agnes, 81
Strype, John, 32
Sturluson, Snorri, 77
Sudbury, Mass., 88
Suffolk, 102, 129

INDEX OF PEOPLE AND PLACES | 181

Sullivan, N Hampshire, 88
Surman, Richard, 39,
Swann, Philip H, 65,
Sylva, Kathy, 152
Sylvester II, 9
Syson, Damon, 152

Tabart, Benjamin, 46, 64
Taylor, Bernard & Elizabeth, 67-68
Tearle, Oliver, 15, 98, 147
Tenniel, John, 157
Tewkesbury, 24
Theatre Royal, London, 10-11, 102-103
Theresa, Maria, 104
Thomas, Bethia, 126
Thomas, Isaiah, 11, 119, 128, 140
Thomas, Katherine Elwes, 9, 13, 14, 19, 31, 34, 46, 57, 63, 93, 109, 117, 124, 131, 132
Thomas, Kelly, 8,
Thomson, Richard, 75, 80
Throckmorton, Nicholas, 64
Tirel, Walter, 144
Topcliffe, Richard, 33,
Toronto Public Library, 153
Tourcoing, Flanders, 159
Traford, John, 113
Tremont St, Boston, Mass., 7
Trevor-Roper, Hugh, 23
Trimmer, Sarah, 95-96
Turner, Rev Baptist Noel, 114
Twiggs, Charles, 103
Twistleton-Wykeham-Fiennes, Geoffrey, 118
Tyler, Mary, 85-90

University College, London, 78, 96

Valley of the Kings, 145
Venice, 113

Verey, David, 21
Verney, Frances, 38
Victoria (Queen), 101, 112, 135
Victoria & Albert Museum, 116,
Virgin Mary, 78, 159
Virginia, USA, 41

Wade, GW & JH, 60
Walker, Diane, 39
Walpole, Robert, 54, 140
Walsingham, Francis, 65
Walton, Isaac, 79
Waltz, Robert, 19
Warbeck, Perkin, 125
Warner, Marina, 157
Warwickshire, 40, 78
Washington DC, 102
Waste, Joan, 133
Waterloo, 102
Watson, Edward, 56
Weir, Alison, 79
Welander, David, 21
Wells, Somerset, 140
Westminster, 80
Westmoreland, 41
Wheeler, Dorothy, 157
Whitechapel, London, 103
Whitehall, London, 124
Whiting, Abbot Richard, 55-56
William I, (Conqueror), 97
William I of Scotland, 44
William II, (Rufus), 144
William IV, 94
Wilton, Wilts, 68
Wilton, Janet, 23
Wiltshire, 68
Winchcombe, Glos, 24
Winchester, 32, 115, 144
Wishart, George, 31-32

Wolsey, Cardinal Thomas, 93-94, 96, 125
Woodcock, Thomas, 44
Woodforde, Rev Christopher, 140
Woodville, Elizabeth, 142
Worcester, 47-48, 159
Worcester, Mass, 11, 119, 120, 140
Worcestershire, 33, 111
Worthing, 88
Wreyford, Paul, 37
Wright, Mr, 53
Wykeham, William of, 115

Yealmpton, Devon, 97
York, 125, 141, 142, 147, 151, 159
Young, Peter, 64

What they said about
Cracking Humpty Dumpty

Brilliant dish

We can discover so much tasty flavour and meaning when we crack into the apparently simple yolk of a nursery rhyme and Tim Devlin's book serves up the dish brilliantly – poached, boiled and fried."

> *Robert Lacey*, author of *Battle of Brothers* and historical consultant to the Netflix TV series *The Crown*.

Marvellous book

I have just finished reading your marvellous book and I can't tell you how impressed I am by it. The research must have been enormous, but you write with such elegance and ease, and with such profound understanding of your subject. I was completely fascinated by it, particularly by the various extraordinary and intriguing identifications of so many important characters — Humpty-Dumpty, Georgie Porgie, Jack and Jill. Really, it is an outstanding work (wonderfully supported by those brilliant illustrations), and like nothing else I have ever read.

> *Selina Hastings*, author and Journalist.

Great Read

Cracking Humpty Dumpty: Great read and super illustrations. Please can I order 4 copies of your next book.

> *Sandy Farmer*, (reader).

Packed with information
Devlin investigate twelve rhymes in detailed depth. He writes smoothly and entertainingly but his book is packed with information. He has consulted dozens of books and other resources dated from 1837 to 2019 and spent hours in libraries and at relevant sites all over the country. It's a pleasantly tactile book too in a nicely designed format by his publisher, Susak Press. The paper is shiny, the font a clear sans serif and the 190 x 240mm size slimly neat.

> *Susan Elkin*, former teacher, journalist and author of several guides to reading and the English language.

Intriguing detective work
This book rounds up 12 of our most popular rhymes and gives intriguing historical detective work, drawn from both primary and secondary sources, plus common sense and imagination, to give us 'most likely' meanings and roots that will often confound the reader.

> *Tim Barton*, Hastings Independent

So scholarly and very readable
Thank you so much for *Cracking Humpty Dumpty* and an advance copy of your next book. Both books are so scholarly and yet very readable. What a detective you are. So myth-busting! I loved the illustrations – delicate and magical. The second book's vision for a national nursery rhyme centre is inspiring and seems to me essential if we are to keep our rich heritage of nursery rhymes alive.

> *Jean Gross CBE*, former government Communication Champion for children, and author of many books on children's learning, including 'Time to Talk', Routledge, 2018.

ACKNOWLEDGEMENTS

I would like to thank **Dr Andrea Immel**, Curator of the Cotsen Children's Library, Princeton University and the staff of the following other libraries for their help with research for this book: the Bodleian Library, the British Library and the London Library. Thank you also to my nephew **Daniel** and his wife **Katarina** for designing, illustrating and publishing it so beautifully and of course my wife **Angela** for her brilliant ideas and editing suggestions.

I would also like to thank the following distinguished teachers, writers and academics who, at the time of this book going to press in May 2024, have welcomed the campaign for a national nursery rhyme centre as outlined in the final chapter (Epilogue) of this book.

NATIONAL NURSERY RHYME CENTRE SUPPORTERS (in alphabetical order)

Professor Roger Beard, former Head of the School of Early Childhood and Primary Education at the University of London's Institute of Education,

Claire Bennett, Founder of World Nursery Rhyme Week and Managing Director of Music Bugs,

Gyles Brandreth, Broadcaster, writer and former politician,

Susie Dent, lexicographer, etymologist and television presenter,

Dr Giovanni Di Liberto, Assistant Professor in Intelligent Systems, School of Computer Science and Statistics, ADAPT Centre and Trinity College Institute of Neuroscience, Trinity College Dublin,

Professor Usha Goswami, Director, Centre for Neuroscience in Education, Cambridge University,

Neil Griffiths, former primary school headteacher creator of the Storysack phenomenon, author of children's picture books, and Director of the National Literacy Project for the Basic Skills Agency.

Jean Gross CBE, former government Communication Champion for children and Director of Every Child A Reader,

Lady Selina Hastings, journalist, author and biographer.

Professor Andrew Holliman, Chair of the Psychology of Education Section of the British Psychological Society.

Dr Andrea Immel, Curator of the Cotsen Children's Library, Princeton University.

Chris Roberts, teacher, London writer and tour guide, author of *Heavy Words Lightly Thrown: The reason behind the Rhyme*.

Professor Kathy Sylva, Professor of Educational Psychology at Oxford University, and leader of the 2004 national study into the effects of pre-school education.

Dame Marina Warner, novelist, critic and cultural historian and author of *No Go the Bogeyman*.

Michelle Windridge, lecturer School of Psychology, Sport and Education, University College Birmingham.

Professor Clare Wood, Director of the Centre for Language, Education and Developmental Inequalities at Nottingham Trent University.